Digital Fantasy Painting Workshop

Digital Fantasy Painting Workshop

MARTIN McKENNA

ILEX

First published in the United Kingdom in 2004 by

I L E X

The Old Candlemakers
West Street, Lewes
East Sussex BN7 2NZ

ILEX is an imprint of The Ilex Press Ltd
Visit us on the web at: www.ilex-press.com

This book was conceived by ILEX, Cambridge, England

Publisher: **Alastair Campbell**
Executive Publisher: **Sophie Collins**
Creative Director: **Peter Bridgewater**
Editorial Director: **Steve Luck**
Editor: **Ben Renow-Clarke**
Design Manager: **Tony Seddon**
Designer: **Alistair Plumb**
Artwork Assistant: **Joanna Clinch**
Commissioning Editor: **Alan Buckingham**
Development Art Director: **Graham Davis**
Technical Art Editor: **Nicholas Rowland**

British Library Cataloguing-in-Publication Data
A catalogue record for this book is available fromthe British Library

ISBN 1-904705-37-5

Printed and bound in China

For more information on this title please visit:
www.ssfauk.web-linked.com

Contents

Introduction

THE ORIGINS OF FANTASY ART are buried deep in our memories and its ideas spring from folklore and mythology, dreams and the more bizarre aspects of reality. Although usually paying close attention to realism, fantasy maintains unreality – the workings of the imagination overpowering the perceived world, creating a suspended or heightened realism.

Fantasy painting has a long tradition. It went through one stylistic revolution in the 1970s and 1980s with the widespread adoption of the airbrush, and another in the last decade of the 20th century with the emergence of Photoshop and 3D modelling. Digital tools and techniques have in some ways made it easier for artists to realize their visions, and the images they are now able to create can often be more vivid, more realistic and more compelling.

This is a book for anyone who has ever looked at a piece of brilliantly executed fantasy artwork and wondered about what techniques were employed in its creation.

In the company of some of the very best fantasy artists working with digital media today, we'll explore all aspects of their individual working methods, and by looking over their shoulders in the form of step-by-step tutorial sequences, we'll discover the exact manner in which their images are produced.

With demonstrations of each artist's individual style and technique, we'll explore artwork from the three great genre categories of fantasy, science fiction and horror.

We'll also very briefly investigate some of the visual traditions of classic genre art in rough-guide introductions, and reveal some of the formative influences of the great

MARTIN McKENNA

FOREST OF DOOM
PHOTOSHOP

'I painted the skin texture for this creature by taking sections from a photograph of a lizard, and then blending them together, and painting them to "sculpt" them into the monster. For the mouth, I again used photographic material to generate the basic form. This was from a photo of a grizzly bear, and after changing it to give it elongated teeth and a serpentine tongue, the mouth has a suitably venomous appearance.'

ROBERTO CAMPUS

'Thanks to the rapid advances in computer graphics technology, we are seeing digital art empowering artists with a new creative tool. It is a tool that in some ways is not yet fully appreciated by some, as they wrongly assume that the computer is creating the artwork instead of the artist himself. Fortunately, as more and more people learn that digital tools are just another way of expressing the boundless creativity of an artist, we professionals in the field can enjoy more recognition and respect. I see more and more artists that once only utilized traditional medias, embracing digital art when they realize that it can provide them with faster production times.'

TODD LOCKWOOD

'I have an uncomfortable relationship with digital painting: it's at once spontaneous and restricting. I find the interface in the Painter program to be great fun, but I don't have an actual painting when I'm done. Because of that, I will always find projects for my oils.'

fantasy artists of the past and the ongoing inspiration of their work, as seen through modern digital interpretations of their styles.

The almost universal transition from traditional to digital techniques in artwork is still new and exciting, and continually evolving. Digital techniques bring an extraordinary freedom to the working methods of artists, allowing much faster production time, more options for alterations and experimentation, as well as better control over preparation for print and far greater ease of distribution. And a great deal less mess.

There are, of course, also disadvantages, which can include the (often literal) headache of staring at a screen for long hours, as well as the very absence of that final physical piece of art and thus the inability to appreciate and sell an original work – which most freelance artists have always relied upon as a major source of income.

FRED GAMBINO

WAYWARD MOON
ELECTRIC IMAGE & PHOTOSHOP
Book cover for Ace books published in the USA.
'I took to working in the virtual realm like a duck to water, and rather than being left behind I was one of the first to produce the kind of work I was doing digitally.... I just enjoy the process much more than working traditionally.'

1

JIM BURNS

'The particular foibles, eccentricities and indeed succulent new facilities offered by, say, the various tools in Photoshop are helping me to evolve my style in a more "organic" direction. I'm finding it very liberating indeed. It's still early days for me with digital art creation. I've done some good things and some iffy things. Time will tell how profoundly the Apple Mac is going to affect my career as a science fiction artist.'

Perhaps the greatest pitfall in digital art, due to the otherwise advantageous ability to infinitely adjust a painting, is the inability to commit to an image, and the ease with which something can be overworked. In fantasy art in general, there is too often a neurotic concern with finish. Successful fantasy art completes itself in the mind of the viewer, done with deft suggestion rather than overworked rendering, achieving convincing results with an economy of suggestion. An overly smooth and detailed digital finish, particularly where 3D rendering is used, can sometimes lead to rather soulless and anonymous results.

Ultimately, digital media can never simply offer a means of avoiding the blood, sweat and midnight oil that need to be poured into the creative processes of picture-making. Artists have simply been provided with a wonderful new set of tools, and to be able to use them to full effect the digital artist will always benefit greatly from having a decent grounding in fundamental art skills.

This book brings together some of the most talented and successful artists in the business. Artists who are at the top of their profession, working in films, computer games, books and comics. A dazzling array of digital artwork produced for *Star Wars*, *Harry Potter*, *Tomb Raider*, *2000AD*, *Warhammer*, *Fighting Fantasy*, *Dungeons & Dragons*, *The Lord of the Rings* and much more, is collected together here. And on the following pages the artists themselves will show you how it was all created.

KARL RICHARDSON

DEATHWATCH
PHOTOSHOP

'Textures and filters don't make a painting; they should simply embellish what is already a good solid piece of work. Good drawing and composition are paramount to a great painting.'

MEL GRANT

SHADOW SORCERESS
PHOTOSHOP

'*Shadow Sorceress*, one of a number of covers I did for the *Spellsong* series by L.E. Modesitt Jr. for Orbit Fantasy Books, is painted entirely digitally so there are no pre-drawings. The female figure was in part made up and in part loosely based on several different scraps of photo reference. The sea scene behind was invented.'

NIKOS KOUTSIS

'Although computer software can be a helpful tool for professional artists, it can be an easy solution for many amateurs who want to do an "okay" job quickly, relying on the use of a few filters or a simple copy and paste technique. As an artist I don't care, but as a professional ... that makes my life difficult in the market sometimes. It's true that computer software makes our lives as artists easier, but basic art skills and a delicate touch are needed before it can be used creatively.'

TODD LOCKWOOD

'You have to know your art skills, and never assume you have anything down "well enough". I can't stress this too strongly, even if you intend to work mostly on computers. You can't depend on computer applications to do your lighting and effects for you. You can't tell when the computer is getting it wrong if you're letting it think for you. Learn what things really look like by painting or drawing them.'

RYAN CHURCH

BLIMP CITY
PAINTER

'This illustration started with a loose idea of upside-down buildings and the types of structures that must be designed to realize that as a concept. I began by working intuitively with translucent media brushes, building up the upside-down pyramidal mega-structure forms and then going in to detail them with their hanging-structure buildings. The painting started out very dark and low-contrast, and only later did I introduce the light source and colour scheme/time of day. Working in Painter, this illustration took about 15 hours to find the design and then add the detail.'

The Creative Process

INSPIRATION FOR FANTASY ART CAN BE FOUND ALMOST ANYWHERE. IDEAS ARE LURKING IN ALL MANNER OF PLACES: IN THE WORK OF OTHER ARTISTS OF ALL KINDS THROUGHOUT HISTORY, IN LITERATURE, FILMS, TELEVISION, AND OTHER MEDIA, DREAMS, MEMORIES, AND IN EVERY ASPECT OF NATURE AND THE WORLD AROUND US.

FRED GAMBINO

Inspiration

Where did you get the idea?

ONE OF THE THINGS THAT I find continually inspiring as an artist, and which lays the foundation for a lot of my own work, is to draw upon stored-up memories of all the potent fantasy imagery that I've retained from childhood. For me, this taps straight into the fantasy films and books which most fascinated and delighted me when I was a kid: the ones that I found scary.

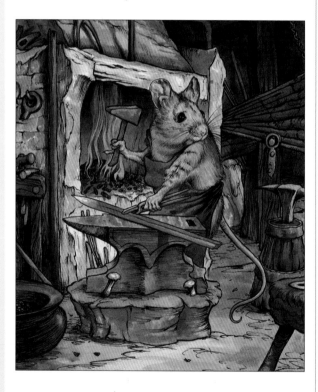

BLUE MOUSE BLACKSMITH
Heavily influenced by the fairy tale illustrations of Arthur Rackham, this picture was done for a children's book. Although more colourful than the darkly atmospheric ink and wash pictures that Rackham created, it echoes his work in many ways, not least by refraining from treating a potentially 'cute' subject with too much sentimentality.

Inspiration also comes from my earliest television viewing, especially the fear generated by the gothic horror stories of *Doctor Who*, with which I grew up. A memorable example from films are the Morlocks in George Pal's *The Time Machine*, which seemed terrifying to me at the time and made a lasting impression.

This motivated me to try to understand and reproduce the feel of what I'd enjoyed so much about that early scary fantasy imagery. Being raised on a diet of Universal and Hammer horror films, and later developing an appreciation of German Expressionism, I've tried to reproduce some of the mood of this imagery in my own work, replicating the use of dramatic light and shade and composition. I suppose that this is why my work often has a melodramatic feel, and a liberal use of heavy shadow and under-lighting often creeps in almost subconsciously.

ON THE JOB

Of course, an artist doesn't always have totally free-rein to let their imagination run loose. When you work in commercial illustration, a commissioned image will almost always be suggested by an art brief for a particular job, and whatever is produced has to fulfil that brief. As a result, there are often constraints to some extent in what can be created, requiring skill to work imaginatively within various parameters. Usually, with luck, there's plenty of inspiration to be found in the brief, or in the source material that it's derived from.

CURSE OF THE MUMMY
Ancient Egypt provides a wealth of strong visual material. Drawing inspiration from the depictions of shambling Mummies in various Universal and Hammer horror films, this figure is given a bit of a twist with the addition of the death mask, based on that of Tutankhamun. A bit of re-styling to make it a half-mask allows us to see the shrivelled flesh of the corpse's face. And, of course, glowing eyes. The statues in the background were based on a photo of a statue at the Great Temple of Ramesses II.

CYBORG
For this cover, I was inspired by an advertisement I saw in a magazine showing a male model looking suitably moody. I'm not sure what the thought process was, but I was inspired to adapt the pose and transform the figure into a blue-skinned cyborg by adding various implants and wires. Almost without realising it, the look of the cyborg was influenced by the Borg in *Star Trek*.

With my own artwork, I actually enjoy working within the confines of a brief. In the creation of an image, I often like my choices to be limited by some factor, and to have my ideas channelled in a certain direction out of necessity. The discipline required in working to a brief is something that I find more productive than being spoilt for choice as to what to draw next.

Often the best images are the product of collaboration between an inspired artist and an equally inspiring art director. A creative partnership of this kind can lead to an artist being pushed a little further, to perhaps reach for something that they hadn't previously attempted, and so bring out the best in their work.

THERE'S A LOT OF IT ABOUT

If we maintain a curious eye, the range of influences that can have an effect on our fantasy artwork never stops growing. Every film we see, every novel or comic book we read, every computer game we play, and every artist whose work excites us, is adding to our own individual visual database, each new discovery increasing the store of ideas our imaginations can run with.

There's a never-ending supply of potentially inspirational material in every direction, and almost inevitably it will sneak into our heads and exert its influence subconsciously. In a search for ideas, the important stuff is whatever fires up our imaginations and makes us want to get creative in the first place.

Reference

What does one of those look like?

REFERENCE MATERIAL CAN BE ENORMOUSLY useful for providing information about an object, a figure or a scene, and for filling the gaps in an artist's knowledge or memory of how something is constructed, and helping to imagine how something might look from a certain angle or under certain lighting conditions.

Some artists use reference far more than others, some not at all. In my own work, I rely on reference photos quite heavily, as I'm usually trying to create representational images that have a reasonably convincing photo-realistic look. With my painted fantasy subjects, I enjoy trying to make them as lifelike as I can, giving them a feeling of being strangely real, as if, for example goblins had somehow been photographed in the midst of a battle, or whatever.

THE HAUNTED LIBRARY

I've always collected useful reference material of all kinds; anything that I think might one day come in handy. And I'm always on the lookout for more. For years, I've cut out and kept potentially useful or inspiring images from magazines, and this archive has grown into an invaluable reference library divided into folders for all kinds of things.

I also keep an extensive library of picture books of all kinds, which has built up over the years. For example, working on fantasy imagery, it's impossible to have too many books offering good picture reference for medieval armour, costume, weaponry and architecture.

But if I still get stuck I'll immediately head down to see what the local public library has to offer. Of course, there are also image searches on the Internet, which is now an indispensable tool for quickly finding reference material.

Using these various sources, I'll always start on a project by getting into the subject of it with plenty of research. Delving into source material helps with creating the right mood and achieving the right mindset for the job — especially if it's a large-scale project such as conceptual design on a computer game, which might involve the recreation of a period in history for which I might be designing the characters, their costumes and weaponry, and various aspects of their world, including its distinctive architecture. If something like this needs to be historically accurate I'll gather together as much material on the period as I can, and refer to it throughout the production. As well as setting the mood, referencing plenty of good source material can spark off lots of visual ideas, and the work itself becomes much more convincing and effective in every way.

BROOM HANDLES & DRESSING GOWNS

Photography has always been the main method of obtaining entirely original reference material. Almost unconsciously, I always keep an eye open for anything useful for artwork I'm planning, or for anything inspirational generally.

In more recent years, digital photography has provided even more versatility. If I'm stuck for a texture or how a

PORTRAIT FOR *RETURN TO FIRETOP MOUNTAIN*

As part of the first step in this book cover design, Duncan assumes the role of the evil warlock Zagor. I hadn't done any preliminary work for the image at this stage, except I knew that I wanted the character's face under-lit and prominent on the cover, as if looming symbolically over Firetop Mountain, perhaps with

his clawed hands clutching either side of the peak. Hence the precise pose.

I worked up a fairly quick pencil rough, and scanned it to add a few digital touches. At this point, I was reminded that the character should have only one hand (according to the plot of the game-book adventure that this cover was for), so that scuppered my plans for any symmetry. I didn't like the idea of having his gristly stump in the picture, but featured it in the rough at this stage anyway, just to get things underway.

After trying various compositions, the image evolved very organically.

Working closely from the reference photograph of Duncan to make maximum use of the information that it provided me with for the lighting on Zagor's face, the addition of some patches of rotted flesh and some nasty stitching completed his resurrected sorcerer look.

certain something should look from a difficult angle, I can often improvise with the use of a household object for a prop, or ask a willing victim to model a particular pose, and the resulting photos are available immediately.

The amount of inspiring material that a good photo-session can give me is amazing, providing so much information and detail that would be difficult, if not impossible, to invent convincingly. Costumes and props can also add much needed extra detail, and they can be nothing more than a dressing gown or blanket for robes and cloaks, or a broom handle for a sword. Carefully lit, the way clothes drape and fold when worn with the model in a certain pose, and how shadows are cast, or the play of light on an object being held at a certain angle, is tremendously

useful information to capture. More realistic elements, such as the more elaborate costumes used in live role-playing events, along with plastic toy guns and rubber swords (or indeed real ones), can only give even more strength to this kind of reference material. The photos themselves can sometimes come remarkably close to the finished imagery I'm setting out to achieve, really helping me to visualize what it is I'm aiming for.

The simple truth is, that in the process of creating convincing fantasy worlds, an artist often needs to be everything at once: a portrait painter and figurative artist, a costume designer, special effects designer, make-up and hair stylist, architect, industrial designer, set designer and lighting director.

Roughs
Preparation of concepts

THE FIRST STEP IN DEVELOPING AN IDEA for an image will almost always involve an initial rough treatment of some kind. This could be a good old-fashioned pencil sketch, a rapid digital drawing or painting, or a rough-and-ready photomontage mock-up – anything that allows a few quick test-runs to try out ideas for colour, composition and so on. This is often an essential part of the creative process, allowing the artist to quickly explore a number of versions before committing to what seems to be the most effective approach to a subject.

The roughs stage is a vital phase on any art job. It allows a visual approach to be communicated with colleagues on a project, or for editors and publishers, who insist on the presentation of at least one rough design, to comment on what an artist has planned. Rapid conceptual drawings also form the basis of any production design process. They help to generate look and feel in the creation of a fully realised fantasy world for any visual media. The concept designs themselves may not warrant any great level of finish beyond a very rough sketch.

ROUGH CONCEPT MONTAGES FOR *FRANKENSTEIN'S LEGIONS*

These are two pieces of rough concept art that were created at speed within Photoshop for the forthcoming computer game *Frankenstein's Legions*. Having been produced extremely rapidly for use as the initial presentation material for the game, they are not at all what I would consider 'finished' images. Nonetheless they manage to quickly convey a lot about the mood and atmosphere of the proposed game, filling in some of the detail about the game's war-torn alternative-history Napoleonic setting.

Each image was created in a couple of hours, using photomontage techniques that incorporated what little Napoleonic reference material that I had immediately available. The idea was to create something that would effectively convey a suitable look and feel for the game concept. It is almost entirely photographic, with just a few Photoshop-painted touches sprinkled here and there, mostly in the background.

For both of the images, the texture of faint lines and cracks, especially affecting the moody skies, was simply created by using a scanned image of scrunched-up tracing paper brought in to Photoshop on a layer set to *Exclusion* blend mode. The intention was to give a sense of antiquity and decay, to help to convey the mood of the game even at this early stage of development.

ROUGH SKETCH FOR *JOURNEY INTO THE VOID*

For this book cover, I began with a sketch of the figures that I wanted to depict in the scene. My personal preference is always to start with traditional pencil drawings. Perhaps this is simply as a result of my long experience in working with traditional media, but I just prefer to start the old-fashioned way – it's still the best way to draw.

Most of the cover roughs I do tend to remain monochrome, which I find is quick to do and conveys a pretty good idea of all the important elements and composition, etc., that I have planned. They also provide an excellent base upon which to construct the final image later. Although I'll have a basic colour palette in mind, I'll indicate this in note form only, as I find it more productive to experiment with colour more fully as I actually start to work on the final version.

This sketch became quite detailed, which is usually unnecessary at this stage, but I enjoyed working on these figures based on my photos of model reference. The drawing would ordinarily contain just enough detail to provide me with sufficient information to start digitally constructing the rough.

I'll then sketch out the separate elements of the composition (perhaps some individual figures, for example) and assemble the scene within Photoshop once these sketches have been scanned.

The final prepared rough (*above-right*) shows how I've integrated the figure sketch into the larger setting. Most of the other elements were also scanned pencil sketches, each sketch being selected and dragged from its original window into this canvas and then positioned as required. For example, I drew only one barrel, but once I had it scanned in I was able to copy and paste it, altering its size and lighting each time to create all of the barrels.

In addition to the basic scans, I drew in various embellishments digitally, using Photoshop's paint tools. Working with monochromatic tones in keeping with the greyscale values of the sketches, I worked on various areas, drawing on top of the scans to fill in details, and painting in the shadows, etc.

Once everything had been adjusted using Photoshop's *Brightness* and *Contrast* tools, the whole scene started to look reasonably cohesive, as though it were all part of a single drawing.

Working this way allows me to construct a scene quickly and easily, and speed is essential in the production of most roughs. The finished rough was enough to show the publisher what I had in mind for this artwork.

The construction of an image

The digital approach to a traditional technique – 'Tradigital'

TRADITIONAL PAINTING TECHNIQUES can be applied very effectively when used within paint programs like Adobe Photoshop or Corel Painter. The latter in particular, as the name would suggest, can lend itself especially well to emulating the look, 'feel' and behaviour of traditional materials. Artists familiar with traditional techniques will find that all the tools and materials they'd expect to find next to their easel are available to use in virtual form.

The paintings here were produced in Photoshop and were intended to achieve a fairly non-digital traditional, or 'tradigital', look. For painting, Photoshop offers three main tools: the *Pencil*, the *Paintbrush* and the *Airbrush*. All apply the chosen foreground colour to the image, and with the use of a graphics tablet and pressure-sensitive pen, the behaviour of the digital pencils and brushes can correspond closely to their real-world counterparts.

MEDIEVAL KNIGHT

1 Using nothing more than the *Airbrush* tool, the figure of the knight is painted on a layer separate to the scanned pencil background, which acts as a guide on which to paint.

2 The details of the knight figure are slowly built up. For reference, I worked from a photo of a museum exhibit.

3 Next, I moved on to painting in the horse. I used the same process as for the knight, blocking in colour and then gradually building up the details.

4 My preference is usually to begin with foreground elements, such as the figure here, and slowly build up detail by painting section by section. Working from foreground to background in this way is the main departure from painting traditionally, where background areas would normally need to be laid down first, usually with foreground elements carefully masked. In fact a much freer approach is generally possible when working digitally.

6 Now the castle can be painted in. Again, I chose to do this on its own layer. The image of the castle itself was inspired by a painting seen in Alan Lee's wonderful book, *Castles*.

5 The sky is painted in on a layer between the background sketch layer and the knight layer, again using the *Airbrush* tool. Working traditionally, this would have been the first area that I would have needed to paint, but Photoshop enabled me to concentrate first on finishing off the knight.

7 The addition of atmospheric wintry trees and a few low-flying crows, along with the horse's breath, completes the scene. Again, a very simple approach to working digitally, using only the *Airbrush* tool (and the *Blur* and *Eraser* tools here and there where necessary), on a total of only four layers.

The construction of an image

Combining photo-manipulation with paint techniques

WHAT'S REAL AND WHAT'S NOT: The obvious step beyond working closely from reference photos, and striving to reproduce their detail in photo-realistic painting, is to incorporate photographic images digitally, manipulating their appearance to work within the artwork itself. This can be a great labour-saving approach in the pursuit of depicting heightened realism, leading to the creation of convincing and very real-looking paintings that are a step closer to bringing fantasy to life.

As a photo-editing program, Photoshop is ideally suited to the manipulation of photos in the creation of fantasy artwork, and by using its sophisticated paint tools, very advanced composites of photomontage and paint techniques can be attained, often making it hard to tell which parts are 'real' photographic areas, and which are entirely painted. It has to be said that integrating photographic material in this way can compromise the hand-crafted feel of wholly painted work, but it depends how it's handled. When photo elements are worked on in combination with fully hand-painted areas, an interesting unity is often obtained, and they can become entirely indistinguishable from each other. These techniques can be a lot of fun to play with, and generally some extremely effective results are achievable much more rapidly than if painting from scratch. Plus it's nice to create a kind of mystery within a digital image, prompting the viewer to wonder exactly what techniques were employed.

I took this digital photo of an old nightclub building, realizing that it would be an ideal model for the spooky, decayed nightclub that featured in a horror story I was illustrating.

I wanted the scene to be set at night, and I thought this setting sun with interesting wispy clouds could easily be turned into a full moon.

In Photoshop, I tidied up the nightclub photo by removing the traffic lights and pedestrian island in the foreground and *Transformed* the building so that a more intimidating perspective was achieved.

SPECTRE

I altered the colours to create a weirder, garish façade to the club, created the 'Spectres' sign using the *Type* tool, and inserted lights into the lanterns on either side. The sunset photo was used on a background layer, with the *Hue* now adjusted to suggest moonlight instead. Lastly, the ghostly snake things were painted in using the *Airbrush*. The whole scene was completed very rapidly.

TRIAL OF CHAMPIONS

The brief for this cover called for a skeleton king on his skeletal mount, charging down a dungeon corridor towards the viewer. I did this rough in my usual way, by scanning in a pencil sketch and adding some quick embellishments digitally. As usual, it also provided a great base on which to construct the image.

This photograph of a mossy stone wall became, rather unsurprisingly, the damp stone walls of the dungeon corridor.

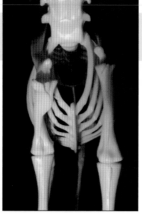

As reference for the horse skeleton, I took several digital photos of a plastic kit I'd built. The information these gave me about the shape of the bones at the angle I required, and the lighting on them, was invaluable. I selected various bone shapes from the photos and incorporated them directly into the image, painting on top of them, adding texture and *Transforming* them to the exact shape that I wanted.

Photographs of armour provided some of the reflections and detailing of the skeleton king's plate mail armour.

This photograph gave me all of the detail that I needed for the horse's skull. I carefully selected it in Photoshop to cut it from its background, and then copied it into the image. I then worked on the basic photo, painting on top of it to adjust the lighting, colour and texture.

The main parts of the horse have been put together at this stage – its leg bones and ribcage from the plastic model kit photos and also the skull photo. The floor of the dungeon is also in place, helping to position the horse's legs along with their shadows.

I took this digital photograph of some rough concrete to use as a quick and simple floor texture for the dungeon corridor.

In the final image, the photo elements have been worked on and adjusted a great deal. Their colour, contrast and lighting have been altered to work in unison with the hand-painted areas, and within the overall image. They've been given greater texture to appear 'aged' and be more in keeping with the subject.

The construction of an image

Combining 2D painting with 3D modelling

2D PAINTING CAN BE VERY EFFECTIVELY combined with 3D modelling by using a hybrid of techniques, as can be seen in the creation of *Lara, my Love* by Danny Geurtsen, which utilized a combination of Photoshop and LightWave.

Initial sketches were done on paper to get a quick feel for the pose of the character. Lara was painted entirely in Photoshop. Her leather belt with the famous gun-holsters, her Uzis and the background were all modelled in 3D using LightWave, rendered out and composited over and behind the 2D painting of Lara. To get the ambience I was looking for, I constantly switched back and forth between Photoshop and LightWave, doing quick rough compositions to see if the separate elements were working in unison, and tweaking the lighting constantly.

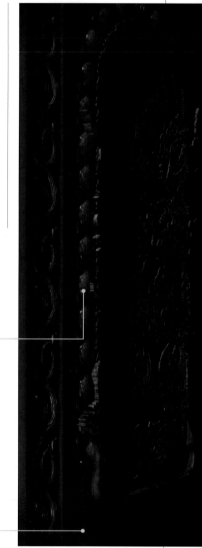

The detail on the doors was realized by painting line drawings of the ornamentation in Photoshop, converting these to selections which, in turn, were converted to a Photoshop *Path*. These were then exported out as Illustrator AI files which Lightwave would read and turn into n-gons. The n-gons were cleaned up and extruded into 3D 'carvings', which were then fitted in place on the doors. Textures for the backgrounds were a combination of a simple painted marble bitmap combined with approximately 7–8 layers of procedural shaders.

Finally, when all the elements were in place, I darkened the corners of the image. I found this literally rounded off the image and fully focused our attention on Lara.

Tomb Raider, Lara Croft and her likeness are trademarks of Core Design Ltd. and Eidos PLC © Eidos 2003

To make the belt and the leg straps work on the figure, I painted skin indentations to make the straps appear tight against her leg muscles. For the guns, it was somewhat trickier, and painting the hands and fingers accurately around the grips of the Uzis took a fair amount of adjustment.

Painting shadows of her fingers onto the grips, with indentations on the fingers, and skin discoloration caused by grip pressure, helped to marry the two elements together.

Barrel smoke was painted to appear as if it was receding into the background, and combined with a trail of 3D bullet shells, this would help emphasize the suggestion of Lara's motion.

The floor decoration was an elaborate Photoshop painting based on Tibetan religious figures. Once completed, it was skewed into place with Photoshop's Transform tools and blended onto the 3D stone floor. The lighting was matched by soft Quick Mask selections and a combination of image adjustment tools (Levels, Curves and Color Balance).

1

The construction of an image

Construction of 3D images

ANOTHER WAY OF CREATING ARTWORK digitally is with the use of 3D graphics, so that rather than applying colour and lines directly with virtual brushes and pens, an artist is applying rules and properties within a modelling program. Instead of creating a surface impression of a three-dimensional scene, the 3D software describes the scene in terms of geometry, lighting properties, surface properties and camera angle.

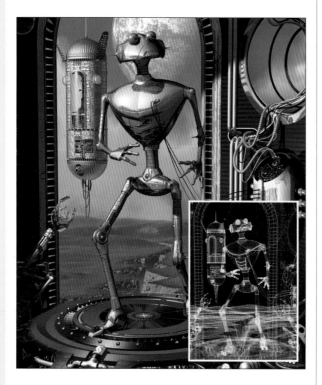

DROID FACTORY
This image was created using 3ds max and Rhino 3D, and was inspired by the famous robot artwork of Hajime Sorayama. The wireframe version of the rendered image is shown as an inset.

3D graphics require the artist to 'build' more than just what's visible, so it's necessary to approach the work with that third dimension – the Z-axis – integral to the thought process, and this is sometimes tricky for an artist familiar with working only in 2D. While this is more complex than drawing a scene, the computer can manipulate a model to make alterations in the 2D image.

So if a view of a fantasy castle were painted two-dimensionally, it might be easier than modelling the scene in 3D, where an artist has to account for things that'll be hidden from view in the final render. Once built, however, it's possible to create an entirely different point of view and alter lighting conditions to generate a new image fairly quickly. A painting would have to be started from scratch to make such major changes.

Particularly in the construction of science fiction machinery, 3D modelling can produce the most satisfying and convincing results – creating spectacular light reflections for glass, metals and plastics with ease. And the incorporation of hardware, such as guns, into an otherwise 2D-painted scene can produce a really effective composite, as seen in the *Lara, My Love* image (*see pages 22–23*).

Fairly rudimentary 3D software programs such as Bryce and Poser are quick to learn, intuitive to use, and can achieve remarkable results. A lot of fantasy artists use these programs as part of the creative process, in the construction of images that are otherwise entirely two-dimensional. Bryce can help in a digital painting with the

STEFFEN SOMMER

ANCIENT SPACE HARBOUR

Created using Maya 3.0 and Photoshop 6.0. The sky and planets are a painted Photoshop background. In the foreground are the ancient docking devices of the spaceport.

creation of fantastic skies and very convincing landscapes. And the figures within Poser can be used as digital mannequins that help with figure reference and lighting decisions for test compositions.

More advanced 3D packages such as 3ds max, LightWave, Cinema 4D and Maya can produce incredible results. For most jobbing freelance artists working in fantasy, the ability to construct many of the key elements of their designs in 3D, including landscapes and architecture, and such hardware as weaponry and

spacecraft, can be a huge advantage. But when it comes to more organic forms, and the human figure and portraiture in particular, many illustrators prefer to continue using a 2D-painted or photomontage approach, as this tends to arrive at more realistic results – and, most importantly, is achievable more quickly than modelling a character in 3D with sufficient detail.

MATT STONE

'3D modelling instantly allowed me to externalize images I've had in my head for years, but was never able to reproduce satisfactorily by other means. In particular, elements using pyrotechnics, smoke, steam and other special effects. For me, I guess the most important thing has been animation – not only could I build stuff, but I could zoom it around, too!'

The construction of an image

The creation of digital black-and-white line art

A BLACK-AND-WHITE DRAWING CREATED digitally with a graphics tablet, within a paint program like Photoshop, can be every bit as effective as anything created using traditional pen-and-ink materials.

The simple process of drawing a black line with Photoshop's tools, such as the *Paintbrush*, *Airbrush* or *Pencil*, can generate fantastic results that are remarkably close to any that are achieved with the use of a drawing pen loaded with black Indian ink. And with the general flexibility that is offered by working digitally, much greater creativity is possible, and the fear and trepidation associated with making totally indelible ink marks on paper are removed from the creative process.

FOR ONCE IT'S BLACK AND WHITE

For most of my early career, I'd been perhaps best-known for my black-and-white line work. I've always loved working with pen-and-ink, attempting to emulate the engravings of great draughtsmen such as Albrecht Dürer and Gustav Doré, and imbuing my work with some semblance of the

CHARACTER DESIGN FOR *MACBETH*

These character design sketches were drawn digitally in Photoshop over a scanned basic pencil rough.

First of all, I adjusted the sketch using *Brightness/ Contrast*, to make the lines as well-defined as possible.

Next I created a new layer on which to work (so as to avoid making irrevocable additions to the scan layer) I started to draw digitally, adding various extra details, using black as the foreground colour with the *Airbrush* at various small brush sizes.

Following this, I then applied a *Gradient* over the whole of each picture, dragging from top to bottom (dark to light), set to *Multiply* mode at 30% *Opacity*, to create the impression of a brooding shadow, with plenty of under-lighting as if cast by a low light source.

This provided an overall grey tone, onto which I drew in various highlights, again using a fine *Airbrush*, but now using white as the foreground colour. The white highlighting enabled me to quickly give the impression of the reflective crown and shiny skin, and to sharply pick out the whites of the eyes, etc., giving a sense of depth and three-dimensions.

TREASURE CHEST

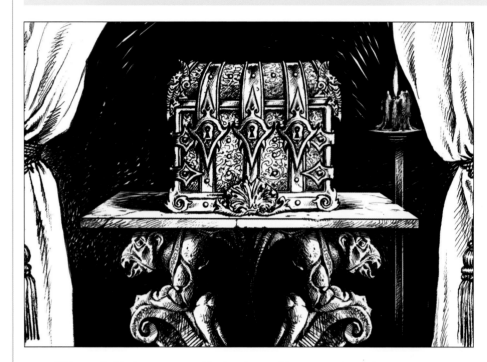

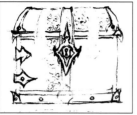

In addition to the black 'ink' lines, I'll also use some white to create the highlights and hatch over the black to create subtle blends that maintain the look of entirely linear and scratchy pen-and-ink drawing techniques.

I'll keep the foreground and background colours set as pure black and pure white, and then switch between them as required.

Working in this way is exactly the same as using a normal drawing pen or brush to apply black Indian ink, while having a tub of process white to hand to apply white highlights and other effects. In fact, it feels a great deal like using scraperboard or scratchboard, but again with much greater freedom.

Of course, another beauty of working digitally in this way is that any repeating elements in the picture need be drawn only once. Only one of the three locks on the treasure chest, for example, needed to be finished; the single lock was then simply selected, copied and pasted into the image another two times. And with the carved gargoyle table legs, only one of these was fully drawn and then simply copied and flipped horizontally using *Transform*.

German Expressionistic light and shade of the Universal horror films I enjoyed so much while growing up.

But outside of comic books, which themselves now rarely appear in black-and-white, it's a fairly niche area of illustration and somewhat overlooked. This is a shame, as black-and-white artwork can have such enormous atmosphere, dynamism and impact.

The creation of black-and-white line work is one of the areas of illustration where digital techniques have an especially distinct advantage over traditional methods, which produce work that is almost impossible to adjust. For me there's no contest, and I'm unlikely to ever return to using my drawing pens and ink (which I think has already long-since dried up in its bottle).

Film production design gallery

ARTISTS CAN FIND THEMSELVES WORKING in a variety of areas, from producing book covers and comics to all aspects of design for games and films. In publishing, painted artwork for the covers of fantasy novels is still in demand, but the current trend is for less representational imagery. This differs from the role-playing games industry, where traditional fantasy artwork remains widespread, for covers and card game art. In the world of comic-books, an artist can work specifically as a penciller, inker or colourist. Computer games and films require a wide range of artwork, and this type of visualization is often produced quickly and remains loose in style. This section explores the film production design work of Dermot Power, for which he predominantly uses Painter.

Cathedral Woods final art

Available on VHS and DVD from Lion's Gate Home Entertainment
© 1999 Babelsberg International Filmproduktion GmbH & Co., Betriebs KG and Hallmark Entertainment Distribution Company

ARTIST **DERMOT POWER** EMAIL **POWER@DIRCON.CO.UK**

Monochrome painting.

Yellow layer.

CATHEDRAL WOODS

Cathedral Woods was done as a production painting for *Alice in Wonderland*. This was mostly created in Photoshop, with some touches in Painter. I painted it in black and white first. I then created three or four colour layers — yellow on layer one, blue on layer two and green on layer three, and so on. The colours need only be approximations of the final colours at this point. I then erased the blue layer to reveal the yellow underneath. Using the *Polygon Lasso* tool, I selected the light shafts, *Feathering* the selection to soften the edges of each shaft of light. Using a large *Eraser* set to 20% *Opacity* I erased the blue layer and the yellow layer underneath, closer to the source of light. A similar technique was used for the shadows on the grass. I could then use the *Hue/Saturation* sliders to adjust the colour on each layer to get exactly the hue and tone that I was looking for.

Erasing blue layer to reveal yellow beneath.

Dermot began his career drawing *Judge Dredd*, and the *Sláine* series *Treasures of Britain*, for the British comic *2000AD*. He began working full time in the film industry in 1997 when he contributed concept designs for Hallmark's *Merlin* TV series. He started working digitally for this project, and has done ever since.

He was asked to join the *Star Wars* concept design team in 1999 on *Episode II*. Since then he's worked on *Harry Potter* and *Batman*, and is currently on Tim Burton's *Charlie and the Chocolate Factory*.

Blue layer.

SCHEHERAZADE FOR HALLMARK'S *ARABIAN NIGHTS*

This image shows the original line and wash art, as well as the finished painting. The director needed to see more of the surrounding environment and so I simply expanded the image to show a wider view of the room's interior.

MANDRAKE ROOT

For this image, a lot of colour was laid in with *Watercolour* before carving the silhouette out with white, keeping the *Opacity* at about 60% so it's not perfectly carved out. Thus the background retains some textural interest.

TEA PARTY FOR *ALICE IN WONDERLAND*

This image was done using a lot of *Watercolour* and the *Smudge* brush to give the whole image a soft and dreamy look. I *Dodged* the shafts of light coming through the trees to give them a hazy, luminous quality.

LEPRECHAUNS

For this production painting, a lot of *Watercolour* was used to bring in texture and dampen the more vivid green tones. The two views show the original line art and the finished painting.

VALHALLA TROLL

An example of how rough an original composition can be. Sometimes it helps to sketch something out at very small scale, then blow it up for a more detailed illustration. This painting was part of a series of images being created for a film pitch. I had to do one picture every day. If I'd had more time, I would probably have thought a little more about the design of the creature and maybe put trees in the foreground and so on ... but it kept its freshness by being stopped before I got a chance to overwork it.

HARRY POTTER AND THE CHAMBER OF SECRETS HOGWARTS

A production painting for the second *Harry Potter* film, created to provide an establishing shot of Hogwarts School of Witchcraft and Wizardry. These images are examples of how useful digital painting is in bringing atmosphere and mood to a miniature. In this case, I was given a photograph of the Hogwarts model on the sound stage, and I painted the landscape around it based on relevant location photographs.

Night-time at Hogwarts

Daytime at Hogwarts

STAR WARS

These *Star Wars Episode II* production paintings began as very scratchy line work done with the 2B pencil in Painter 6, followed by painting on a *Gel* layer to allow the lines to remain visible. The backgrounds were done with a *Rake* brush These were painted very much in the style I liked to employ when painting comic books using traditional media. I used flat brushes with opaque paint and gel layers as digital 'glazes'. These images were done as quickly as I could, to keep them fresh. Often the problem with

Sith for *Star Wars Episode II*

digital work is that you can endlessly polish a picture and tighten up the details to a point where it gets stale. I like to move on when I feel I am getting bored. It's also important to note that I am not trying to recreate the look of paint as you see it in the real

Sith for *Star Wars Episode II*

world. I am simply making an image that pleases me. It just so happens that many of the marks I make, even when using digital methods, are more often than not the kind of marks that also result from traditional painting and drawing methods.

Padme for *Star Wars Episode II*

FAIRY CASTLE

This was an image that I did in Painter almost entirely using *Watercolour*, because *Watercolour* stays separate from the artwork until it is 'dried'. I could build up the clouds and blend them with my line work as a guide, then erase the line art before finally drying the *Watercolour*.

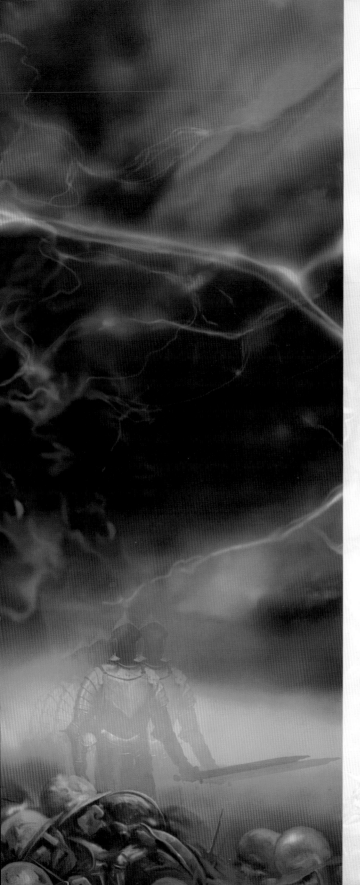

Realms of Fantasy

Fantasy imagery has popped up in various forms throughout the history of art. It can be found in the symbolic landscapes of Hieronymus Bosch, in the work of visionary artists such as William Blake, and surrealist masters such as Salvador Dalí. But it's fantasy literature that has inspired most of the archetypal fantasy art of the last couple of hundred years.

FANTASY ART CAN PROVIDE a seductive escape-route into a world of our own making; a way of blurring the borderline between the external reality that we all share, and an individual artist's mental landscape. Fantasy artists can give substance and reality to whatever whims inspire them. They're constrained only by their own imaginations (and very likely by an art brief and an impossibly tight deadline, too).

An early pioneer of fantasy art whose work I find fascinating was Jean-Ignace-Isidore Gerard. He produced delightfully weird and whimsical engravings for his own story *Un Autre Monde* (*Another World*) in 1844 under the name of J. J. Grandville. His endlessly imaginative illustrations were influential, inspiring the more fantastical aspects of Gustav Doré's art, notably for *Baron Munchausen*, as well as the work of Sir John Tenniel, whose brilliant illustrations were the first to bring life to Lewis Carroll's *Alice's Adventures in Wonderland* and *Through the Looking Glass*.

Another prolific and influential illustrator of that period was Arthur Rackham. He's always been one my particular

A panel from *The Garden of Earthly Delights*, by Hieronymus Bosch c.1500. Essentially a medieval religious artist with a strong satirical bent, he was one of the great masters of fantasy painting.

Baba Yaga travelled in a mortar, rowing the air with a pestle and sweeping her tracks away with a broom. An illustration from 1902 by Ivan Bilibin for *Stories: Vasilisa the Beautiful.*

favourites. Rackham's pen and ink and watercolour illustrations are wonderfully sombre and atmospheric. His drawings of goblins, fairies and weird, twisted trees have had a lasting influence, and their effect can be seen in the work of many of the best modern-day artists working in fantasy, including Charles Vess, Brian Froud and Alan Lee.

J. Allen St. John is another artist who has played a vitally important role in the evolution of fantasy art. His work appeared in the early pulps like *Weird Tales* and *Amazing Stories* in the 1930s and 1940s, most notably illustrating stories by Edgar Rice Burroughs. Worked in oils in a style reminiscent of Rubens, St. John's covers were filled with energy and excitement, and through them he devised the whole look of heroic fantasy. His work paved the way for later painters such as Roy Krenkel and especially Frank Frazetta, who has been one of fantasy's most important and influential artists. His epic *Conan the Barbarian* and *Death Dealer* covers have become icons of the genre.

Frazetta's style has been endlessly imitated, defining the look of the 'Sword and Sorcery' sub-genre since the 1960s, his barbarian heroes and heroines influencing the work of later artists such as Jeff Jones, Ken Kelly, Rowena Morrill, and Boris Vallejo.

A *Weird Tales* cover from 1933 by J. Allen St. John. The forerunner of Frazetta and Vallejo, St. John established the look of 'Sword and Sorcery'.

Traces of Frazetta's style continue to appear, having influenced the look of Simon Bisley's work on *Sláine*, which itself has had a significant ongoing effect in recent years.

Perhaps the first fantasy paintings I saw that really wowed me as a kid were on the covers of the UK *Fighting Fantasy* game-books in the early 1980s. These featured artwork by Peter Jones, Les Edwards, Ian Miller and Chris Achilleos, whose work I'd loved from years before on the Target *Doctor Who* covers. Most special of all, I thought, were the wonderful watercolour paintings of Iain McCaig. His cover for *The Forest of Doom* was one of the first painted fantasy images to make me stop and stare, and later his paintings for *Casket of Souls* were beyond amazing.

The *Fighting Fantasy* books were all part of the fantasy games explosion that started with *Dungeons & Dragons*, and which has given rise to masses of fantasy art ever since the mid-1970s. Some of the most established artists best known for their game-related work include Jeff Easley, Larry Elmore and Keith Parkinson. It seems game art in particular has defined the exact look of elves, goblins and the other usual races, developed from the generic Tolkien-inspired blueprint. Lots of talented artists have emerged from this very productive area, but RPG-related material is perhaps to blame for a kind of bland 'medieval America'

Death Dealer, by Frank Frazetta, was originally the cover image to *Flashing Swords #2*, edited by Lin Carter. This is one of Frazetta's most celebrated pictures, and it is rightfully considered to be a masterpiece of the fantasy genre.

imagery that has seemed all too common in fantasy art over the past several years.

My list of personal favourites goes on and on, and there is a vast body of work that has made me resolve never to stop improving my own skills. We're barely scratching the surface of a rich and inspirational genre of fantasy painting.

Castle Siege

THIS IMAGE WAS CREATED as a production painting, used as part of the development process on a medieval RTS (real-time strategy) game called *Plague*, which I worked on at Eidos Interactive. I produced several conceptual paintings of this sort, which were intended to help flesh out some of the character and detail of the gritty and dirty medieval world that formed the game's background. With these paintings I needed to inject some colour and atmosphere into the overall development of the in-game visuals and attempt to add a little depth to the game's medieval setting – in part to help the other artists working on the project to realize the mood of the late-medieval period we were striving to recreate. But they were more than just inspirational – it was also intended that this sequence of paintings would eventually be used to illustrate the manual accompanying the game, and also potentially as loading screens within the game itself.

SOFTWARE **PHOTOSHOP** ARTIST **MARTIN MCKENNA** WEBSITE **WWW.MARTINMCKENNA.NET** EMAIL **MARTIN@MARTINMCKENNA.NET**

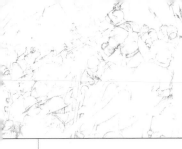

1 I began this picture by sketching out the basic scene in pencil on some ordinary cartridge paper, which I then scanned into the computer. The details of the image were inspired and influenced by a variety of source material, but in particular the composition was heavily influenced by the subtle, yet

spectacular, watercolour battle scene *The Holy Wars of Charlemagne,* by Alan Lee. Found in his beautiful book, *Castles,* this has been a source of inspiration for many years. The details of the figures and their armour and costume were informed by the superb photographs of medieval re-enactment in Gerry Embleton and John Howe's book, *The Medieval Soldier,* which was an invaluable guide to many of the costume designs for the *Plague* game.

2 With the scanned pencil sketch as the background layer, I started to lay down some colour by using the *Airbrush* set to about 60% *Opacity,* on a separate layer opened on top. This very quickly and loosely established a bit of the background colour, and provided a little something for the figures to be painted against.

3 With the artwork I was doing on this project, and with all my digital work at this time generally, I was very keen to maintain a traditional look to my paintings and so I more or less took a traditional approach to the methods I used. Working digitally allows a good deal more freedom, of course, and I was able to leap forward, and start painting in the figures at an early stage, without having completed any of the background as yet. Using the *Airbrush* with a hard-edged brush, I blocked-in the flat colours of the figures

and worked-in some of the surrounding shadows to paint against. On a separate layer, I used the *Line* tool to start establishing the shapes of the halberds' wooden shafts, erasing the sections where the soldiers' hands were positioned.

4 I now started to apply some darker values to the areas of flat colour, so that they would begin to shape the areas of shadow, such as the folds in the clothing and the darker patches on the helmets. Using the *Smudge* tool, in a technique similar to that used in traditional oil painting, I blended the different tonal

values to sculpt the details in the cloth folds and to suggest the reflections of the metal helmets. I also introduced a few lighter tones to add detail to the helmets, defining their metal ridges and rivets. The final thing that I did at this point was to model the skin tones and the details of the faces quite closely. If the composition allows it, I often like to very nearly finish a section of a painting before moving on to start on a neighbouring section, and so on, working section by section throughout the picture, as this step-by-step shows.

5 On a new layer, I followed the same process for the next section of painting. This stage is where I block-in the colours with a hard-edged *Airbrush,* and apply some darker and lighter values, which I then blend together using the *Smudge* tool to achieve the desired shapes and forms. I added various finishing highlights to define some details in the metal reflections, and so on.

I opened a new layer to work on this section – just for my own peace of mind – so that if I did anything that I was entirely unhappy with, I could then simply drag the layer to the bin and start painting afresh. Luckily, this wasn't necessary. At this point in the process, I also started to strengthen some of the halberd shafts and other straight edges using the *Line* tool.

6 I now moved on to another section and painted in the next figure. I started painting him on a third layer, sandwiched between the previous two layers, as he had to appear behind elements of the foreground figures but have his halberd thrust in front of the first ones that I'd painted at the start. After completing this little area, I merged the second and third layers together, and then on a new layer above, I started to paint in the big metal claw in the foreground, using Photoshop's *Line* tool.

8 With all the details on the knight complete, I now worked on the shields on another separate layer. I referred to historical reference to make the shield designs reasonably accurate. I painted on various stains and scuffs to make them look a bit used, in addition to having an arrow or two embedded in one of them. I also blocked-in the shadows below the shields and painted in a glimpse of the helmet of a soldier who is climbing the ladder. On the metal claw layer, I finished painting all the details of its shadows and shiny highlights.

7 This image shows the flat colours that I started with in the construction of the knight on the battlements. Again, I began this figure on a new layer. The same technique for the metal armour was used as before, with fairly crudely applied flat colours of appropriate values simply blocked-in with the *Airbrush*, and then blended and refined using the *Smudge* tool.

9 On another layer, I introduced some of the background figures on the right, including silhouettes of soldiers with halberds to suggest a bit of distance. At this point, I also started to block-in the castle wall on the right, as well as the top of the siege ladder. Now I also chose to add a heraldic design to the tabards of the earlier figures for impact, and to make the edges of their clothing appear a little battle-dirtied and tattered and frayed, to add more visual interest and drama to the image.

10 Now I started to add detail to the castle wall, using the *Smudge* tool to blend darker values that I'd applied with the *Airbrush*, to form the outlines and texture of the stone blocks, and adding lighter values to highlight their upper edges a little. On another layer, I painted in the details of the spear lying across the top of the battlements, and the hand trying

to push the ladder away. I also painted in the detail of the wood of the ladder, blending light and dark lines to suggest the wood grain. In the background, I introduced a little more colour to the sky and painted in a haze of smoke, again with a large soft *Airbrush* at about 60%, partially obscuring the silhouettes of the soldiers at the rear. On a separate layer, I also painted in the first of a hail of arrows being fired over the walls. I did these quickly, using the *Line* tool, at each end rapidly painting on the arrow heads and flights.

12 The picture's now almost complete. All the elements have been painted in; the siege tower has been adjusted so it has stronger shadows; and the final figures, including the knight carrying the white banner, have been painted in front of it. I added a chain, running diagonally across the bottom left corner of the picture, to suggest the suspension of another platform out of sight in the foreground, upon which the main

group of figures have arrived at the castle walls and climbed up from. The chain was created on its own layer, very simply by applying a round blob of dark colour with a hard-edged brush and erasing the centre of the blob with a smaller brush to make it look like a chain-link ring. Applying appropriate highlights to it, I simply copied and pasted this many times to create the chain and used the *Line* tool to link them together.

11 A big step forward, having painted in the basic colours for the siege engine looming into view on the left. This wooden tower and platform was painted again with the hard-edged *Airbrush*, the paint then moved around and blended with the *Smudge* tool. This part of the composition was most heavily

influenced by the Alan Lee painting. Also, the figures locked in combat in the centre of the picture were now lightly painted semi-opaque, along with the white banner with chevron design. These elements were kept quite pale and translucent, to suggest their distance and immersion in the clouds of battle smoke.

13 In the final image, the *Brightness* and *Contrast* were adjusted to make the picture a little less bright and crisp, and a slight *Gradient* in *Multiply* mode was applied to darken things down a little farther, and to make the atmosphere seem a bit smokier and gloomier. In all, this painting was created entirely 'by hand' within Photoshop, using extremely simple methods that remained reasonably close to traditional painting techniques, utilizing, for the most part, only the *Airbrush*, *Smudge*, *Eraser* and *Line* tools. No filters were used,

and only a very small amount of adjustment was carried out, using *Brightness/Contrast* with a little finishing touch from the *Gradient* tool. All in all, the resulting image is something that fits the 'tradigital' description very well.

Magic Time

IAIN **M**C**C**AIG **IS KNOWN** as a feature film artistic director, concept designer and filmmaker. He was one of the principal designers on *Star Wars Episodes I, II* and *III,* and has worked as concept designer/storyboard artist on *Peter Pan*, *Harry Potter 4*, *Interview with the Vampire*, *Terminator 2* and many other films. Iain is also a widely published illustrator specializing in narrative and figurative art. His illustration work includes book and record covers, limited edition prints, posters, advertising and children's books. Here Iain shows us his approach to painting digitally, combining traditional drawing with Photoshop techniques, in the creation of the cover for the book *Magic Time 3: Ghostlands*, and the box art for the *War of the Ring* game.

DIGITAL ARTWORK: MIND THE GAP

'Working as a concept designer in films can be a little frustrating to your inner artist. "May I see some of your work?" people ask, and not only can you not show them anything you've done for the last couple of years unless the film has come out, but you also won't be able to show them what you're doing on the current film until many more years have passed. The transition from my virgin never-touched-a-computer-before years and my current screwed-if-the-power-goes-out way of painting lies in one of those gaps. Correction, if the power goes out, I spend the ubiquitous hour staring at my brushes wondering which end to use, and then I get on with it. Okay? I can still paint. But with paint paint, I struggle with the medium. With digital paint, I only struggle with my ideas.

'The blinding speed of digital painting is God's gift to artists. Of course, digital painting can also take forever, since you can change your mind over and over and over again. The resulting mush is not a pretty sight. Usually. Some artists have the right kind of brain for it. Not me'.

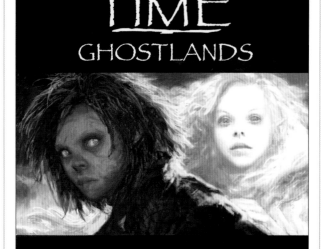

ROUGHS 1, 2 AND 3

I was concept-designing the characters for the author at the same time as trying to create an image for the cover. Inigo was the tough one, beautiful but hideously ugly at the same time. I was all over the map on him. The publisher also was concerned that the cover not look too juvenile. That's great news when you've got two kids on the front cover. Eventually, everyone seemed happy with a combination of number 1 and number 2, but less juvenile. These are Photoshop sketches, all the way. Two layers, one for the image, one for the border. Lots of coffee.

1 Background first. Fill a layer with black and go to town with the *Airbrush* tool. Blur with *Motion Blur, Rubber Stamp* bits over other bits, make a mess. I knew it would barely show in the final, but I needed something spooky to paint into.

2 I sketched this face onto the back of an envelope in front of the computer and then scanned it in. I put it on a layer on top of the background, and erased the envelope.

3 Then I simply added the details. Lots and lots of *Multiplying* colour into the pencil drawing, and then painting on top to blend out pencil. The rest is just lots of art school training. The trick to making Inigo ugly but beautiful was to have a good-looking face and paint it horrible colours and grisly textures. And then add lots of hair. Hair makes almost anything look cute.

4 Cut Inigo out and paint Tina in underneath. I fizzed her into the background with a little *Airbrush*, then adjusted Levels to push up the contrast between the two characters. A colleague told me once that if your painting isn't working, it's probably your contrast. My tendency is to paint everything with equal fascination and end up making wallpaper. I've learned that dark shadows and blank spaces are there to give your eye a chance to rest. Ironically, digital art tends to suffer from the wallpaper syndrome. Equally ironically, it's the quickest digital fix of all.

5 I checked the cover with the border and type (always my topmost layer) and then resized the image a little smaller to let it breathe. I showed Step 4 to the publisher and the author for their opinions. The former thought that it was still too juvenile, and the author worried that the main characters seemed disconnected from each other. I suddenly realized that Tina and Inigo's body language was all wrong. Actually, I didn't suddenly realize anything. I spent several days thinking I should get another job and leave painting to real artists. Then I scooched Tina's body around towards Inigo and put her hand on his back and the intimacy instantly connected the two characters and stopped it from looking too juvenile. And there was much rejoicing.

War of the Ring

'**S**O HERE'S THE WAY **I** PAINT on the computer today. I have two studios (I'm old, I deserve it). One has an easel and several drawing boards and smells like an art school. The other has a G4 with a 20" monitor, a Wacom tablet and a scanner, and the strongest smell in here is my shampoo. I start in Studio A (the traditional one). *War of the Ring* is a box cover for a game by Universal Vivendi. Or rather, two box covers. You can play either the good guys or the bad guys in this game, so the concept was to have a "Good" and an "Evil" cover. On the good cover, an elf stands with an orc head under his arm. On the evil cover, the orc's got the elf's head.'

SOFTWARE **PHOTOSHOP**   ARTIST **IAIN MCCAIG**   WEBSITE **WWW.IAINMCCAIG.COM**   EMAIL **IAIN@IAINMCCAIG.COM**

2

ROUGHS

I scribble the idea down and sent, it off to the client. I'd put the characters against white, as if you'd yanked them, dripping and blinking off the battlefield, straight into a photographer's studio. The client approves the concept of the severed heads, but wants the two covers to join up, and asks me to put a stormy sky in the background, as well as the battle-crazed armies of the orcs and the elves.

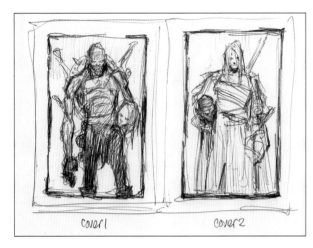

1 The stormy sky. I run to Studio B (the digital one) and paint this sky in Photoshop. I make squishy brush noises and play heavy metal, to get as much passion into it as possible. Norman Rockwell once said that creating a painting was like bouncing a ball off a wall; it never comes back as hard as you threw it. So throw hard. I painted the clouds in black and white to get my tones right, and added a little *Motion Blur* just because.

2 Back to Studio A, where I draw the two armies, in pencil, on paper. Why don't I just do this on the computer? I do, sometimes. Not today, though, maybe I needed the exercise. Back to Studio B, I scan the art, save it to another layer. *Multiply* this layer into background clouds. Add a little *Motion Blur* (and why not?).

3 Another day, another layer. I begin in the same way as the day before, except this time it's the elf and the orc. I spend many hours in Studio A, posing strangely clad in the mirror and trying to draw with my free hand. I think I may have even photographed myself at one point, which is a little embarrassing, because I don't have a digital camera yet and still have to go to the developers. Swear I'll hire models, one day. I cut these guys out and leave them on a normal layer above the background. My underpainting is complete. Time to paint.

4 Splish, splash, when will digital brushes make noises? On a new layer, I drop a green wash over the whole thing and begin to block in my tones on another layer above that. This is about halfway through, and it's all about the joy of colour.

5 With the blocking-in now complete, I start to finish off the orc: using another layer when I'm feeling cowardly, and then flattening it when I'm feeling brave. Brave is better. Always.

6 Bouncing back and forth between the orc and the elf, I notice that I've made the heads under each arm the same, so I change them. Also, I hate that big blank spot between the two characters, so I paint the Eye of Sauron with a ringlike lens flare while I'm 'waiting for the paint to dry' (technology has ruined a lot of great excuses).

7 Get serious on the elf time. They say the last ten per cent is halfway there. No digital tricks here, just blood, sweat and midnight oil as I paint the last ten per cent of the elf. Actually, there is one trick, but it's so stupid I'm embarrassed mentioning it. The pommel of the sword has an entire Elvin poem embossed into it (scanned lettering, warped around the pommel and embossed using the appropriate filters). I like hiding things in paintings, all right. (I know, seek therapy.)

8 At the last minute, the client suggested that perhaps red is a more appropriate war colour than green. This is where digital paint scores, big time. I zip back and turn off the green wash (except on the figures) and try various red to orange *Gradients* until I find something suitably aggressive. I *Airbrush* a layer of orange dust on the horizon line and, at the client's suggestion, cut and paste heads on the orc so the snarly one is under the elf's arm. And there it is done, finished, the end. Almost. I forgot to mention that on a topmost layer I always keep the final framing with text and borders, and it would be remiss of me not to show you that too. So...

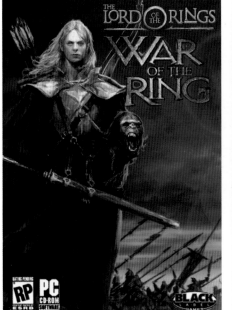

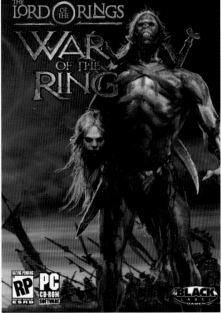

9 Here it is all finished. Now go home and paint.

Death Throne

MELVYN GRANT has worked continuously as an artist in illustration in the UK, Europe and in the USA, with all the major publishers. His projects range from children's books and posters through adult romance, science fiction, fantasy and horror, but science-fantasy is his speciality. Though he prefers working on books, he has also worked in advertising, animated films, prints, gift designs and record sleeves. Until seven years ago, he worked entirely with oil paint on canvas or board. Now most of his commercial work is painted digitally, as he prefers the drying speed of pixels.

Mel's approach to digital painting adheres very closely to the traditional oil painting techniques he used prior to his transition to working digitally, and he has now fully embraced digital media, as he explains: 'I've always considered myself an artist, not an illustrator, although I do illustrations. When I first painted professionally, I experimented extensively, trying to find the perfect medium to specialize in — each had an advantage that appealed. But no one medium had everything. So I spent a lot of time going from one media to another and never quite finding what I wanted. It was a frustrating time.

'The idea of having a machine to help me do most of the work had always been a dream lurking in the back of my mind. At that time, computers were very expensive and not up to much anyway. So I went completely the other way and came round to oil painting. Oils seemed to fit the bill nicely: there was the drying time of course, but that was something I could live with. Naturally there were still little

THE GNOME IN A TREE
I had a 4x5in transparency of this oil painting that was used as a book cover for an edition of *Grimm's Fairy Tales*, which I scanned in and used as the basis for the background of *The Curious Wizard* (*see page 49*).

MELVYN GRANT IS REPRESENTED BY CHRISTINE ISTEED OF ARTIST PARTNERS, LONDON.
WEBSITE WWW.ARTISTPARTNERS.COM EMAIL CHRIS@ARTISTPARTNERS.DEMON.CO.UK

things that irked – nothing is perfect – but on the whole it was okay. My work became labour-intensive, as painting is, but it was most satisfying and I gained a lot of skills of which I am now very glad.

'And then the digital revolution came along, and and my paintbrushes have since remained stuck to the wall. Working digitally is as near to the perfect medium. It has everything rolled into one. But computers can sometimes be demanding little beasts and come with all kinds of problems and frustrations. Crashing in the middle of a desperate deadline is their favoured move. That's when it's a good time to know something about the technical side, or know someone obliging who does.

'I've never used 3D programs or entirely computer-generated stuff in any of my work. I'm interested only in doing good digital paintings in as "hands on" and as natural and easy a way as possible. All I've done is swap oil paint and canvas for pixel and screen and I like to stick as close as I can to the techniques I used in traditional painting – the way I worked prior to my affair with digitalization.

THE TECHNICAL STUFF

'The program I use is Adobe Photoshop and sometimes Painter. They are the only programs I've found that are suitable. Painter would seem the natural choice, but I keep coming back to Photoshop. If Painter were a smaller and faster program just for painting, as its name suggests, without all the other stuff it's cluttered up with, it'd be great. Photoshop is also the "industry standard" for the printing world and is straightforward. The perfect program would be an "artist's" version of Photoshop, including an improved Painter-styled brushes plug-in.

THE CURIOUS WIZARD

This is a hybrid picture done for the fun of it. The main character was worked around one from a group of gnomes in another of my paintings, called The Master's Learning Chair. I removed his hat and gave him dreads with beads and a satchel. The background was based on an oil painting that I did some time ago (see page 48), but I changed it a lot, including the colours, and completely repainted it digitally. The robin and the additional branches were made up.

2

'Meanwhile back in the humble digital art studio – the first "must have" thing to stick into your computer is a digitizing tablet. It's the only way to accurately shift around all those pretty little pixels. All my artwork is painted into the computer using an A4+ (12x12in) Wacom tablet. A mouse is no good. Not even a laser mouse. As for the mouse pen, which I tried a long time ago, that's worse.

HERE WE GO

'First off, when starting a new piece of art, I do whatever research is necessary and gather whatever reference I need: photos, or sketches, or whatever. And reference is important, even if it's only a good long look at something. It can always be put aside, and then subconsciously used, or even forgotten and something completely different done.

'After all this preparation, I get out the sketchpad and start the preliminary drawings. Sometimes I use a standard pencil, sometimes a blue pencil (I like blue) and sometimes a bunch of coloured pencils, or something else – whatever grabs me at the time. And maybe a sketch later I have my start. But mostly, after many tired sketches, and much irritability and frustrated sore-headedness later, I scan it in'.

'Once it's in the computer, I can adjust the format and work up any parts that need a little more attention. This has now become my layout for the painting and if this is a personal piece, I just get straight on with it. If it is a commissioned piece, it is at this stage that it goes before the art director, usually as an e-mailed low-resolution JPEG file. Often it then goes on further and is presented at a weekly meeting and its here that more decisions about it are made. It then comes back to me, and after several deep breaths I make any changes wanted. After this, I go to final

art. Now it's mine again. I just get in there and do it. Painting and blending, I work colour and detail over the whole canvas, building it up to the final touches. The tools I favour most are the *Brush* tool, occasionally the *Airbrush*, and the *Smudge* tool.

'Sometimes I use the layers facility in Photoshop and sometimes I just paint it flat. The beauty of layers is that you can select a portion of your art as a layer, work it up, duplicate it, change it, and compare it. If you don't like it – bin it, dupe it and go round again. The possibilities in painting digitally are almost endless and there are few rules here that can't be broken. Just enjoy the program, but do read the program manual first. It can save a lot of hair-tearing. And a word of warning here: always remember to save your work *often*.

"Then at some time, I'm aware that the painting is just about finished. I email a low-res to the client again, just in case. Fine. Okay, now I whack it onto a CD and send the high-res version off and it's done. The final art is a Photoshop PSD or TIFF file (depending on which the client asks for) at 360dpi in CMYK and RGB mode (I like to give a choice). I always work in RGB with the CMYK view on and with CMYK compatible colours. A small point here, that's bigger than you think: if you're working in RGB, make sure the colours are compatible with CMYK – especially the blues – as they change when converted. That beautiful bright ultramarine could print as a dull slate grey. Photoshop has a little tag in the RGB sliders that appears in the bottom left corner when a colour is not compatible. Just click on it and the colour will adjust. When I'm painting in the computer, I like it to feel, as near as I can, like I'm slapping some oil paint onto a canvas and

The Kiss of Medusa

smearing it around – or using watercolours, pastels, pencils, acrylics, dirt, dung or cosmetics (yes I have painted with such things, well not dung ... yet) – whatever.

'Blending colour to me is like being able to fly and I have flown with most mediums at some time or other, but oil paint in particular gave me a deep satisfaction, and digital is the same. Anything that I can paint digitally, I can do in oils more or less, and vice versa. And that pleases me greatly. But the same skills and hard work must go into digital art as any other art if something worth looking at is to be created. And before even touching a computer, *learn to draw* – there is no way of avoiding this; and you also need to develop an accurate eye. Just because you are

THE KISS OF MEDUSA

This piece was done as a digital experiment when I first tried creating final art on a Mac. I based the images on pieces of photo reference that I had lying around at the time, and this is the only time that I have used a Photoshop Lens Flare filter. I never really thought much more about this piece, but a lot of people seem to like it very much.

using a computer, don't think there's an easy ride here. You must still be able to see how your subject is really constructed and have the ability to put it down on paper, or screen, or something to keep. All the Old Masters had this capability and all the new and Future Masters will have developed these same basic skills. And so must you if you are going to achieve anything at all, whatever medium, digital or otherwise.'

IN **THIS STEP-BY-STEP, MEL** demonstrates his very traditional techniques applied to painting digitally: a truly 'tradigital' approach. 'This painting was commissioned by Wizard Books for the cover of Ian Livingstone's *Deathtrap Dungeon* Fighting Fantasy gamebook. It's a straightforward digital painting, and I had a lot of fun doing it, and this is a step-by-step guide to its creation.

'Apart from the original sketch, which was done with a soft blue Caran d'Ache pencil on a page from a cheap A3 sketchpad bought from my local stationers, this piece was painted entirely in the computer via a Wacom A4+ tablet using the Adobe Photoshop program. The Photoshop Tools I used were the *Paintbrush*, the *Airbrush* occasionally, and the finger *Smudge* tool. The *Paintbrush* puts on the colour and the *Smudge* tool blends it, just like in oil painting. The *Airbrush* is to help with any large smooth area that I can't do with the *Smudge* tool. I also used the *Paint Bucket* tool on basic background colour. I didn't need to do any research for this piece, as I'm quite familiar with warriors, armour, and the odd skull and rat. Anything I didn't know, I made up.'

1 This is the original sketch using blue pencil on an A3 sketchpad. There were two pre-attempts before this sketch, but they were screwed up into little balls and, the last I heard, were the property of my neighbour's tomcat.

2 The sketch has been scanned into Photoshop, positioned, and then the background extended and sized to the book jacket format. The faint border around the picture is on a separate layer and covers the extra area that will be added to the final painting to allow some bleed for the printers to trim off to the finished book size (otherwise they'd chop off a bit all around my painting). At this stage, I sent it to the client for their approval.

3 Here I have changed the background tone to something more suitable and started to work in the colour. I have also reshaped part of the helmet. The coloured dots in the upper left are part of my palette and have been placed on a separate layer. They will be removed when the art is done. Ignore the toilet roll; that was me being childish.

5 Now the overall mood is further developed and the finer details are added, including cobwebs and the fallen shin-guard. I like to work the whole painting up to where it is waiting for those final few touches that make it complete. And just like eating the cherry last, those touches are the most satisfying. My approach is the same as building a house. Work from the ground up. You can't put on the roof before you have built the foundations.

4 Now I have worked in more colour and detail. All of the major work is done and the feel of the painting is about right. It is at this stage that I know the painting is on-course and I start to bring out the finer details.

6 This is the finished piece of art ready for the client – complete with added rats, at the author's request.

7 This is the painting as it is now. I went on to change the colours and add little touches here and there, including remodelling the throne somewhat. It has been one of those pieces that I have looked at and thought maybe I'll just change this bit. I half feel like adding a couple of nubile women, lurking in the shadows somewhere … semi-naked of course. But I'll probably just leave it as it is for now.

To sum up, any advice that I have for the would-be digital artist boils down to these few points: become a good draughtsman first, have lots of good ideas and don't be afraid to put in plenty of perspiration. There is no way around having to learn to draw well, planning everything out properly and getting all of your reference up-front – also cram as much RAM as you can into the machine you work on. But most of all, have fun with your art.

Fire and Ice

AFTER A SUCCESSFUL CAREER as a commercial artist working in the advertising industry, Todd Lockwood was astonished to be told that people were willing to pay for the fantasy and science fiction art that he vastly preferred to create. That discovery altered the course of his life, and he is now one of the most widely respected fantasy artists working in the field today. Known worldwide for his depictions of heroic and stirring high-fantasy imagery for such publishers as TSR and Wizards of the Coast, he also creates works of great sensitivity and beauty in quieter styles. Well over a hundred paintings from all areas of his fantasy creation are collected together in his beautiful book *Transitions*, published by Paper Tiger, which can be purchased from his website.

'I like to work digitally in much the same way that I paint in oils: I work with transparent washes or glazes that don't obscure my drawing too much until I have fully discovered all the relationships. Then I add detail and fine-tune things with combinations of glazes in the shadows and opaque colour in the highlights, working back and forth until everything is in balance'.

Here Todd shows us his techniques using Painter and takes us through the creation of *Fire and Ice*, a cover painting he produced for the *Dungeons & Dragons* miniatures game, *Chainmail*, published by Wizards of the Coast.

1 This is a gesture drawing that I then based a photo-shoot on using live models. In this sketch, I'm just looking for the interaction of lines in the two characters. This is done in Painter with the *Pencil* tool.

SOFTWARE **PAINTER**   ARTIST **TODD LOCKWOOD**   WEBSITE **WWW.TODDLOCKWOOD.COM**   EMAIL **TODD@TODDLOCKWOOD.COM**

2 This is the same drawing after the photo-shoot, with the characters being fleshed out and with some blending done to model the forms. I still used the *Pencil* tool for this, but I am also now using one of the blending brushes, called *Grainy Water*. It's a good tool, because you can use it to blend edges that pick up the texture of the ground. The paper can be controlled for roughness and contrast with a slider.

2a This image shows how the brush is selected in the menu.

2b Here's how the *Papers* palette looks after picking a brush. At the bottom of the picture are sliders for *Scale*, *Contrast* and *Brightness*.

2c This screengrab shows the *Scale* and *Contrast* sliders cranked way up. It was basically by turning the texture and contrast up that I did the metal texture on the Iron Golem in one of my other paintings, *The Iron Fortress*. Then I turned it down again to paint on. There are various paper textures to choose from, and you can create your own, although I haven't done that as yet.

3 Here I've laid in some water-colour washes to add a little colour to everything, and removed some of the highlights using the *Wet Eraser*, one of the *Digital Water Colour* brushes.

2a

2b

2c

3a

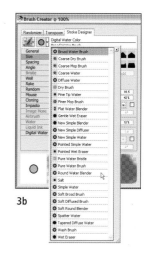

3b

3a This shows the *Broad Water Brush* that I use for these glazes, with its settings.

3b This image shows the other brushes in the *Digital Water Colour Brush* menu. The *Pure Water Brush* blends and softens, and the *Wet Eraser* removes color. The *Round Water Blender* adds a different color fairly softly into wet colour that is already down.

2

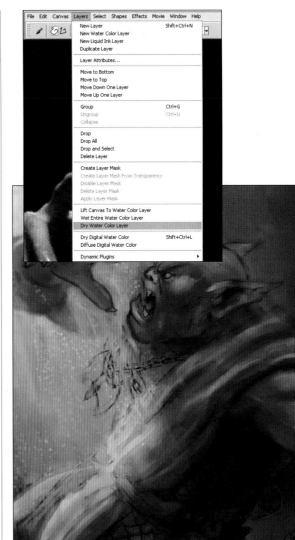

4 This is where I start on the actual 'painting' as such. The sky is in pretty quickly, and the rock forms happen fast – a couple of hours in all. Although you will see that it gets tweaked here and there, it doesn't change much from this point on.

5 This is how the Half-Dragon progresses. The foreground fills in, and the dragon skull gets some early modelling. I'm about to start on the Hobgoblin, and it was really for this figure that I took most of the reference snapshots earlier.

6 The Hobgoblin under-painting was done, up to this point, pretty much entirely with the *Digital Water Colour* brushes that I've already demonstrated. This meant using the *Broad Water Brush* to lay down layers of transparent colour, and then the *Wet Eraser* or *Round Water Blender* on one end of my stylus to wipe out the highlights, and the *Pure Water Brush* on the other to soften and move tone around. In Painter, when you have a layer of wet paint finished to a level that you want to keep, you go up to the *Layers* menu and select the *Dry Water Colour Layer* command (*see image above*). The *Water Brushes* are the only ones that are transparent, so these are the ones that can be used as 'glazes'.

7 Here, I am laying in some new glazes, to feel my way into the flesh tones for this guy. Hobgoblins are supposed to have red skin, but I don't want a ton of red in a picture I am seeing as mostly neutral, so I am going to sneak up to the chroma that works for me.

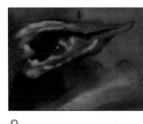

8 The first view is zoomed in on the Hobgoblin's ear to show how the initial highlight colour is laid down on top. Some more highlights are then blocked in onto the Hobgoblin's forehead and finally, they are blended with the *Grainy Water* brush. The work moves quickly at this point because I can make one end of

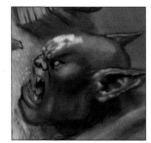

my stylus be the paint brush, and the other end the blending brush. What saves the most time in Painter is two things: drying time and paint mixing. The 'paint' is always dry or always wet, in essence, as needed. The pallet is 'point-and-shoot', and it is just

so easy to re-do that last dab a little darker, or a little less saturated, a little greener and so on. Since you can continuously pile layers of paint on top of layers, it's very easy to build up to the bright centres of those important highlights.

7a

7a This is a screengrab of the settings of the brush that I use most often for 'opaque' work. I created it myself, following the step-by-step in the manual, and have found that it works pretty well for me most of the time. I could have named it anything I wanted. I lamely named it *Round Pointed*. Now that I have established the values of the middle tones and shadows more or less, I will start adding opaque highlights.

9 I continue adding opaque highlights, work back and forth with opaques and glazes, and come fairly quickly to the end. His tabard is pretty loose. His arms didn't need much more than some spots of colour glaze and a little tightening here and there. His armour is little more than some bright highlights on top of the initial glazed under-painting. The drawing is clearly

visible. The illusion of real paint holds together pretty well, even close-up, especially considering that what you see at 100% is probably twice as big on a monitor as what I would have painted in oils for the same cover. You can work in a way that feels pretty loose and gestural, and still come up with something that is very tight in the end.

Archer's Death

NIKOS KOUTSIS IS A RESPECTED AND highly successful freelance illustrator in his home country of Greece, and he has worked professionally in the fields of advertising and magazine editorial since 1991. Nikos has worked as a cartoon animator for the top Greek production company Stefi Films, as a concept artist for McCann Erickson in Athens, and for Disney in Paris. Since turning freelance, Nikos has created cartoon logos for Cosmocarta (Cosmote) and Top Kid (Dannone), and has worked as editorial illustrator for top-selling lifestyle magazines like *Nitro*. More recently, Nikos has been creating comics for magazines such as the Greek *PC Magazine,* and has been preparing his own comic book, co-created with SF writer Michalis Manolios, whose stories are the perfect inspiration for Nikos' fantasy art. *Archer's Death* was created as a promotional piece for display at a RPG-Comics Convention, and demonstrates Nikos' comic-book painting techniques using Photoshop.

'I'm a Mac user, and I continue to produce a lot of my 2D art using an aging copy of Adobe Photoshop 4. Although evolution is a good thing, I'm extremely comfortable with this older version of the program, and it's perfectly adequate for the work that I do. Some later-version tools offer more versatility, but I find it distracting to try to stay up to date constantly when my priority is to spend as much time as I can in my real-world studio at the drawing board, working with pencils and paper. Not that the Wacom tablet isn't an amazing tool to have on my desk, but I prefer to use it in the application of colour, while the feel of my pencils still gives me the most satisfaction in my monochrome sketch work.

'Let's see what we do after having spent a few hours (or all through the night when the deadline is looming) preparing the pencil art. To prepare the pencil sketches for digital painting successfully, the scanning steps are crucial to lay the correct foundations.'

SOFTWARE **PHOTOSHOP**   ARTIST **NIKOS KOUTSIS**   WEBSITE **WWW.KOUTSIS.COM**   EMAIL **NKOUTSIS@OTENET.GR**

1 First, simply place your
artwork on the flatbed scanner.
The Preview feature and the
scanner's *Marquee* tool will allow
you to view and frame the desired
area to be scanned.

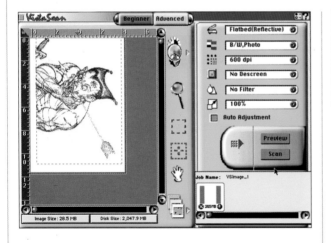

2 Now, set your scanner to use
its greyscale mode (displayed as
B/W, Photo on this scanner) and
a *Resolution* of 600dpi. You will
soon reduce that resolution to
300ppi, but initially you need
your scanner to read the
maximum amount of information
in order to achieve the best
possible line quality.

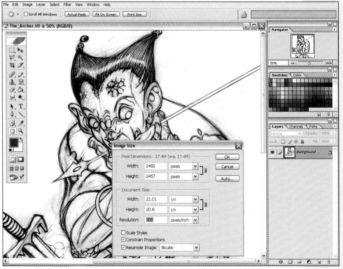

3 Now that you have your
image available to you for
opening up in Photoshop, these
are the steps that you have to
take to prepare a completely crisp
and clean image to work on.

Begin by going to *Menu > Image >
Image Size* and reducing your
image to 300ppi. While you're
there, you should also check that
the image proportions are set to
those that you require.

2

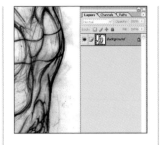

4 All around your pencil lines, you'll see specks, dots and grey spotted areas that you'd probably like to get rid of. And if you've used a soft pencil to prepare your sketch (something like a Faber Castell B, like I used for the art you see here), then you need to select *Image > Adjust > **Levels*** or ***Brightness/Contrast*** and make some tonal adjustments using the sliders. And if that doesn't fully do the trick, select the *Brush* tool from Photoshop's *Tools* palette, with white as your foreground colour, and finish the job manually, making sure at this point to save your image!

Convert the image to colour mode using *Image > Mode > **RGB Color***. It's now ready for any of the millions of colour selections available to use in your painting. To prepare your art for print, it has to be in CMYK mode, which is a more cumbersome file to work with and which doesn't allow you to use many of the software filters you might need, so the image is best worked on in RGB. The RGB mode is used only for on-screen productions (Web, TV, etc.) and presents some non-printable colours, so you need CMYK Preview (*View > **CMYK Preview***) while working on the image to be aware of what you'll get in the end. Just remember to convert your RGB file to CMYK for print.

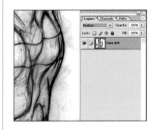

5 Right now, your only layer (check the *Layers* palette) should be the *Background* layer.

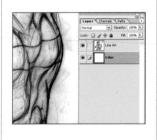

6 Make it a common layer by double-clicking on it, give it a name such as 'Line Art' and convert it to *Multiply* mode in the *Layers* palette options. This will make all of the white areas transparent and whatever is created beneath it (which will be the colouring) will be visible.

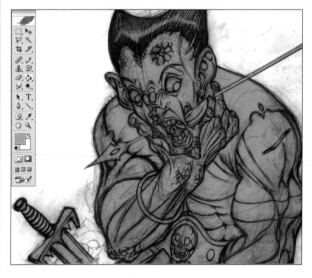

7 The big trick I employ in my work is to colour under the greyscale lines. Create a new layer, name it 'Colour' and drag it beneath your line art layer. Now you're ready to get painting.

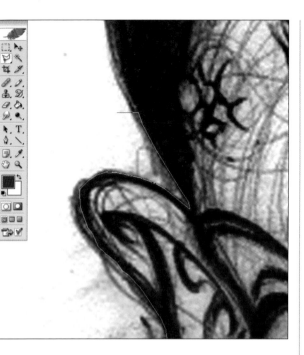

8 Begin by using the *Lasso* tool on your 'Colour' layer, beneath the greyscale lines, to select the outline of the first area of your drawing that you wish to add some colour to.

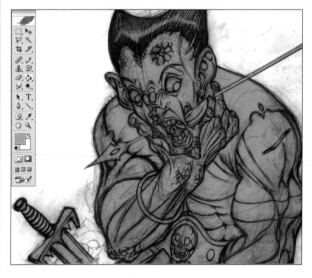

9 Once you've made the selection, fill it with a flat colour by using the *Paint Bucket* tool from the tool bar.

10 Then, still using the *Lasso* tool, continue selecting the large areas, then the smaller ones, and finish by tidying up the remaining details.

11 From time to time, *Hide* your line art layer and zoom in on the artwork to make sure you don't leave uncoloured spots here and there. If you find any, you can always fill them using the *Pencil* tool. A very simple technique, but one that is very effective.

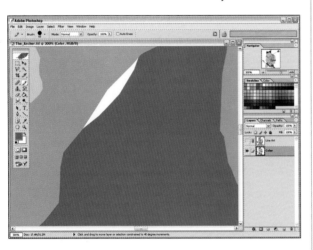

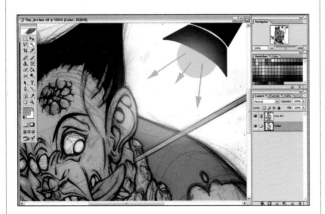

12 Define where the light source is: this is a must. Then choose the *Magic Wand* tool and go through the image selecting any areas that you want to add highlights or shadows to.

13 Now using the *Airbrush*, apply paint in those selected areas. In the *Brushes* palette, choose the *Screen Mode* (for highlighting) or the *Multiply Mode* (for shadows). Also, set the *Control* option to *Pen Pressure* and lower the *Opacity* to about 55%. Start airbrushing softly over the selected areas you want to apply shadows or highlights in.

14 When you feel satisfied with the result, follow the same process, choosing all the other areas one by one until you're done with all the main elements. Painting within a few more smaller selections inside the already airbrushed areas, using the same process, will give a greater three-dimensional sense of depth and form.

15 Now you're almost done. Using the *Magic Wand* tool and selecting any desired area, you can use *Image > Adjust > **Levels*** or *Image > Adjust > **Color Balance*** to make any tonal or colour adjustments you like. Just experiment and see what effects you achieve. Also, adding a filter or two like *Blur* in some selected areas will provide a result like that of the almost finished image. Finally, *Flatten Image* in the *Layers* palette will complete the job. Don't forget to convert that RGB file to a CMYK one and save it as a TIFF format for print.

Darkblade

KEV HOPGOOD IS A BRITISH ILLUSTRATOR and cartoonist based in Bromley, Kent. In the 1980s and early 1990s, he specialized in artwork for many science fiction and fantasy comics, including contributions to well-known titles such as *Iron Man* and *2000AD*.

In recent years, he has moved into computer-based design and illustration, working first for leading computer games company Psygnosis, and latterly as a freelancer. He now specializes in children's and editorial illustration, working for clients such as *The Guardian*, Oxford University Press and Games Workshop, for whom he continues to work on the popular *Darkblade* character.

Here Kev demonstrates his techniques, using Photoshop and Painter, in the creation of a monochrome comic strip page for *Darkblade*.

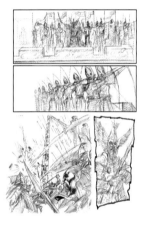

1 I pencil the page using traditional pencil and paper. Some artists work directly on the computer, but I find this perfectly adequate for laying down visual ideas. Once I'm happy with the layout, I scan the pencils in at 300dpi and tidy up the panel borders in Photoshop. I select the individual panels and save them as an alpha channel. This makes them easy to select later. I also stroke this selection to form the panel borders on a separate layer.

2 I do the lettering in Illustrator. The pencil page is imported as a template layer and the word balloons and captions artworked. There are a lot of comic lettering fonts available now. I use one called *Whizbang*. Back in Photoshop, I cut and paste each panel into its own file, so I can concentrate on artworking one panel at a time.

SOFTWARE **PHOTOSHOP, PAINTER, ILLUSTRATOR**　ARTIST **KEV HOPGOOD**　WEBSITE **WWW.KEVHOPGOOD.CO.UK**　EMAIL **KEV@KEVHOPGOOD.DEMON.CO.UK**

3 I fill each panel with 50% white to knock it back a bit and open the file up in Painter. On a separate layer, I trace the pencil art using the *Scratchboard* brush, which is a variant of the *Pens* tool. The effect is one of tracing on layout paper or acetate, with the advantage that you can just *Control-Z* if you screw up. In fact, I find myself mentally thinking *Control-Z* when I'm drawing with pencil and paper.

4 When I've finished the line work of the foreground, I take the file back into Photoshop and make a selection of the foreground using the *Magic Wand* tool. Painter has its own magic wand tool, but I find that the Photoshop version is far superior. I usually have both programs running at the same time and go back and forth between them. Next, I fill the selection with a flat tone, covering up the underlying pencil and making a base to paint over with Painter's excellent brushes. Although Photoshop is catching up, Painter still has superior natural media painting tools.

I tend to go for *Gouache, Watercolour* and *Oil Pastel* tools to build up the tones and model the figures. Once I'm happy with the individual panels, I then paste them back into the page in Photoshop, flatten the file and save it out as an EPS. Working digitally has freed up my drawing and put me in control of more aspects of the overall look of the artwork. The only downside that I can see is that there is no final art created to sell at comic shops and conventions. Selling prints is all well and good, but I think punters often prefer to own something that the artist has actually sweated over.

Snap

KRISTEN **P**ERRY **WORKS PRIMARILY** as a texture artist on such computer game projects as *Counterstrike* and *Team Fortress 2*, for Valve Software. Kristen also creates fantasy posters in collaboration with the web comic *Megatokyo*, and she produces fine-art prints of her other paintings. In this scene, painted using Photoshop, a Japanese warrior in kimono garb walks through a snow-covered forest. A snap breaks the silence, setting off a flutter of birds to her side, and she reaches for her katana. In this tutorial, Kristen focuses on the creation of an extremely detailed and realistic leather texture. She demonstrates the use of displacement maps, blend modes and adjustment layers used in the painting of this character's beautifully rendered kimono obi-belt and skirt.

PART ONE: CREATING THE INITIAL SHADING

1 Brush a neutral solid colour to cover all areas where the leather will be. Once you have the shape mapped out with a medium tone of the colour of leather you desire, lock the layer to keep this shape clean for future additions.

2 With a hard-edged brush, roughly put in the highlights and shadow tones according to the light source of your piece. Don't worry about being exact, since this is just for placement. Note the slight shadow edge next to the highlight edge.

SOFTWARE **PHOTOSHOP** ARTIST **KRISTEN PERRY** WEBSITE **WWW.MEREKATCREATIONS.COM** EMAIL **MEREKAT@MEREKATCREATIONS.COM**

3 Taking a softer, fuzzy brush, work in the folds and smooth out the lines created with the highlight. Using a warmer tone that is somewhere between the base and highlight colours will help soften the edges further. Ideally, the pressure sensitivity of a tablet will be the most help, but if necessary, simply using various-sized fuzzy brushes on a lower *Opacity* to build up the tones will suffice just as well.

4 At this point in the process, adding reflective light and supplemental highlights with another soft brush will add some variety of colour to the base tones. Since my environment largely consists of golds and blues, I use those colours lightly. The blues are the reflection of the sky bouncing off the snow.

5 A good universal way to deepen the colours once base tones are in is to apply a levels adjustment. Hit *Ctrl + L* to bring up the *Levels* window and move the left arrow at the base of the graph right and the right arrow a bit left. My numbers happened to be 26, 1.00, 243 for this step.

PART TWO: CREATING THE LEATHER TEXTURE

6 Create a new RGB document the size of all of the leather that you need to texture. Next, pick two brown colours, a lighter medium and a darker medium, and make sure that they are set as your foreground and background colours in your *Tools* palette. Add clouds (*Filter > Render > Clouds*) until you achieve a nice pattern, something with an even distribution and not too much noise.

7 Duplicate the layer and add more clouds to get a new pattern (*Ctrl + F* will duplicate the last filter used). Set this second layer to the *Darken* layer blend mode and decrease the *Opacity* slightly. This will even out the blotches and give a more complex pattern. Copy merged (*Ctrl + Shift + C*) and paste into a new layer. Add noise (*Filter > Noise > **Add Noise***). I set mine at *3.96, Gaussian Distribution*, with *Monochromatic* checked. Flatten and save as 'leathertexture.psd'.

8 *Ctrl + click* on your shaded leather layer to make a selection. Add a mask of the exact shape to itself (bottom of the *Layers* pallet, click on the grey square with a circle in it to add the mask). This will help later. *Duplicate* this shaded leather layer (and its mask) into a new document with its mode set to *Grayscale* (*Image > Mode > **Grayscale***) and a background of 50% grey. *Auto level* the shaded leather layer (*Ctrl + Shift + L*) and *Desaturate* (*Ctrl + Shift + U*). Use *Levels* again to tweak the tones so the overall base of the leather is a 50% grey and only highlights and shadows remain. Save the document with its layers and mask as 'displacementlayers.psd'. Copy merged into a new greyscale file. Flatten the file. Save the greyscale document as 'displacementmap.psd'.

2

9 Go back to 'leathertexture.psd' and apply a *Displacement Map* (*Filter > Distort > Displace*). I used these settings: 80% *Horizontal Scale*, 100% *Vertical Scale*, *Stretch To Fit* and *Repeat Edge Pixels*. Photoshop will then open up a window asking for the displacement map. Choose your 'displacementmap.psd' and click *OK*. It will distort the leather

according to the highlights and shadows that you saved in the greyscale file earlier. White and black tones will result in various high/low extremes of movement while the greys offer less distortion. a setting of 50% grey will give no distortion. Next, open your 'displacementlayers.psd' and copy the layer with the mask on into the final distorted leather layer. Following that, select and apply the mask to the leather layer, then delete the greyscale distortion layer. You now have the final leather distortion with its own mask. I've tinted the mask area to more easily view the folding of the leather.

Note: make sure the leather file is the same size as the distortion file, or else the resulting distortion leather mapping will be improperly scaled for your artwork. If necessary, simply scale the leather to the same dimensions before displacing.

10 Copy the final distorted leather layer into your artwork and align it with your subject. Since you have the mask applied to the layer, the outlines of your leather distortion make aligning easier. Apply the mask, if desired. Change the distortion layer's blend mode to *Lighten*. Adjust with *Levels* if necessary to make it more pronounced. Duplicate the layer, add a mask to this new layer, apply the *Clouds* filter to the mask and set the layer's blending mode to *Darken*. *Desaturate* to taste. This adds discoloration to the mottling of the leather and adds interest as if it is slightly worn.

PART THREE: FINAL TOUCHES

11 For the final touches, I used a combination of three additional layers. To make things simpler, you may want to flatten all of the leather layers into one layer before adding these, but it is not necessary. For demonstration purposes, I have shown the layers in their 'normal' blend mode state so that the brush strokes can be easily seen. In practice, be sure to create the layers with the colours that are in the blend modes listed in steps 12–15. Make these adjustment layers by *Ctrl + Alt + left clicking* on the edge between the two layers (the cursor will change to two stacked black-and-white circles). Adjustment layers allow additions to be shown only within the confines of the pixels on the base layer. It's sort of a quick and dirty mask without the clutter. They will help when you do handwork on associate layers.

12 The first layer is an 'overlay' layer that is set to about 26% *Opacity* and which consists of blues and whites that were painted with a large fuzzy brush.

13 Next is a 'scumbling' layer, in which I took a small brush and an olive colour and basically scribbled over the texture, adding cracks and a pattern similar to skin.

14 There is no real technique to the scumbling, just a lot of henscratching. However, when this layer is set to the *Multiply* blend mode at full *Opacity*, the olive colour blends beautifully to create a nice texture.

15 Finally, I add a *Highlights* layer set to *Hard Light* at an *Opacity* of about 59%. This layer consists of teals and oranges and is meant to bring out the highlights of leather folds, both from sunlight and reflective light.

16 For final details, it's just a matter of bringing out some more of the sunlight in highlights, shadows and reflective lights to dull down the colour. For this, I've applied two final layers: one a *Colour* layer set to 85%, in which I added some medium-deep greyish teal to the under places where reflective light would be; the final layer is a simple *Multiply* layer for the shadows created by her arms and folds. And that's it.

Atlantis

THE *ATLANTIS* IMAGE WAS CREATED BY Alan Giana for his own enjoyment and as a portfolio piece. Alan has always been inspired by the sea and sea life, and marine mammals in particular. He wanted to create a painting that had a magical feeling to it, yet be real enough that the viewer could imagine this scene really existing.

Born and raised in Connecticut, Alan Giana always wanted to be an artist. With a degree in graphic design, Alan started his own business, Giana Graphx, in the early 1990s.

Through the years, Alan has worked on a variety of illustration and design projects. His artwork has appeared on book covers, magazines, children's games and music CDs, and has been published in several books and magazines showcasing the best in airbrush and digital illustration. He has won many awards, including the Pro-Comm Award of Excellence by the Business Marketing Association, the Premier Print Award by the Printing Industries of America and the Oppenheim Toy Portfolio Best Toy Award. Alan's paintings have been displayed in numerous galleries and shows around the USA.

Alan's love of nature and the sea has always been a big part of his life. His appreciation for the beauty that surrounds us, even in our own backyards, plays an important part in the artwork he creates.

Alan says of digital work: 'Creating artwork digitally offers an artist the ability to create, explore and play with composition fairly easily. This is particularly helpful when working on an illustration assignment and the client wants to make changes. If done correctly, the artist won't have to go back to the drawing board so to speak. These changes can be made to an element on a particular layer without affecting the artwork below it, and this will save the artist a lot of time and aggravation.'

SOFTWARE PHOTOSHOP, PAINTER, FREEHAND ARTIST ALAN GIANA WEBSITE WWW.ALANGIANA.COM EMAIL GIANA@PCNET.COM

2 Here I added in the ancient ruins and columns structure, which was inspired by a photo that my sister took while she was on vacation in Italy. This was created as a separate file using Photoshop and then brought into the existing background image on a new layer. I then created a new layer on top of the columns structure and filled it with solid blue. I then faded back the *Opacity* of the layer to create the illusion that the columns were being seen through water, and this made them more distant in the scene.

1 This shows the background of the painting, which was created using Photoshop and Painter software. All painting was done using a Wacom drawing tablet and stylus. The water was created in Painter using the *Airbrush* tool, and then the wave effects were created using the *Gooey Distortion Brush* set to *Bulge*. Distant coral and reef effects were created using the *F/X Brush* set to *Fire*. The rocks in the front were created from a reference photo I took while on vacation in the desert in Arizona. I faded back the rocks to create the illusion that they were further back in the scene.

3 I added bubble effects in front of the columns, using the *Airbrush* tool in Photoshop set to *Dissolve* to get a misty effect, and also set to *Normal* for the larger individual bubbles. I added some distant fish shapes in the background as well in front of the columns.

4 The dolphin was created as a separate illustration in Photoshop. The basic shapes of the dolphin were drawn in FreeHand and brought into Photoshop as *Paths*. Each path shape was used as a mask or frisket so that I could work on individual fins and portions of the dolphin without affecting the other parts. The shading was created simply using the *Airbrush* tool in Photoshop.

After the dolphin was finished, it was brought into the master painting file on a separate layer so I could position it accordingly in the composition.

5 I followed the same steps to create the other dolphins and added them to the master painting file on their own layers.

7 I created the moorish idol fish in the same manner as the dolphins and other fish, and brought it into the master painting on its own layer.

6 I painted the foreground reef in Photoshop using the *Airbrush* tool with various brush settings and shapes. I created butterfly fish in the same manner as the dolphins, and brought them into the master file on their own layer.

8 Finally, I added some bubbles coming out of the small dolphin in the background by using the *Airbrush* tool set to the *Dissolve* and *Normal* settings.

Well of Darkness

THIS IMAGE WAS CREATED for the wrap-around cover of a fantasy novel called *Well of Darkness*, the first in *The Sovereign Stone* trilogy, published by HarperCollins. It started life as a very basic brief from the publisher's art editor. It showed the three principal characters from the book appearing in a kind of tableau, with a king on his throne at the centre, a prince dressed in ornate black armour to his right and an apprentice wizard to his left. All three are posed together in a small group against a background of an ornate castle door. Some initial rough sketches helped me lay out the scene and establish the position of the decorative columns on the extreme left and right of the picture, as well as in the centre of the image to define the area of the book's spine.

The image was constructed in four component parts: one for the background, and one for each of the three characters in the group. Only at the very end were they finally assembled in the composition.

SOFTWARE **PHOTOSHOP** ARTIST **MARTIN MCKENNA** WEBSITE **WWW.MARTINMCKENNA.NET** EMAIL **MARTIN@MARTINMCKENNA.NET**

1 This initial concept sketch from the publisher was a suggested variation on some of my very early pencil concepts, and it established the basic grouping of three central characters. With this composition to plan around, I arranged a photo-shoot with models, to help with figure reference.

2 This first pencil rough was assembled in Photoshop from separate drawings of the background and the three individual characters. At such an early stage, the drawings can be scanned at low resolution.

WORKING AT PRINT RESOLUTION
As the final image was for print, the resolution had to be fairly high – at least 300dpi. This made the image size very large (4205 pixels wide x 3011 high), and thus quite cumbersome to manipulate quickly within Photoshop. Working on separate pictorial elements in their own individual canvases helps to lighten the overall load. The king, for example, was created on a much smaller canvas, just 576 pixels wide x 1023 high.

3 I now needed to fine-tune the scale. The three characters in this sketch were drawn separately, so I hadn't worried about their being in scale with each other as I drew them, allowing me a little more freedom in their execution. Once scanned, however, each figure was carefully selected with the *Lasso* tool, and the selection was then refined using the *Paintbrush* and *Eraser* tools whilst inside the *Quick Mask* mode.

The figures were dragged from their canvas using the *Move* tool and dropped into separate layers on the background. They were then adjusted using *Transform* to ensure that they were in the correct scale and position.

4 I now moved on to my pencil sketch of the king. Having completed any necessary *Transform* adjustments to the position and scale of the king, I used the separate sketch of him as a base to start painting. I created a new layer – with a resolution of 300dpi – on top of the sketch layer. Keeping the painted work in its own layers makes the eventual extraction of the final colour image much easier.

5 It was now time to paint the king. Photoshop's basic paint tools were used to work up all of the details for this character on separate layers and to create a more 'tradigital' painted look. The *Burn* tool was also used in one or two areas to increase contrast. Other adjustments were achieved with *Image > Adjust > Brightness/Contrast*.

6 The same basic process applied to the figure of the prince. The initial sketch was kept in its own canvas and worked on separately from the rest of the main picture. Again, I created a new layer on which to apply the colour work, keeping the sketch as the background layer.

2

7 I was now ready to paint the prince. This character's facial features were built up by using Photoshop's paint tools. The stylized design of his armour was meant to suggest the appearance of a flayed body, with muscle and bone worked in metal. Individual areas of the figure were carefully masked off to contain the application of airbrushed colour. Each mask was created using the *Lasso* tool, and then the *Airbrush* and *Eraser* tools were used within *Quick Mask* mode to ensure absolute accuracy.

8 The pencil sketch for the character of the apprentice wizard was given exactly the same treatment as were the other two characters. The ability to concentrate on just the single figure separately in this way helped in working up all of the detail that gives him his character and individuality.

9 It was now time to move on to painting the wizard. I wanted to depict him in his brown apprentice robes in the midst of spell-casting, so I gave him an appropriate conjuring pose. In the novel, he is described as

having a large, distinctive purple birthmark on his face, so I painted in that detail, too. Everything was painted using Photoshop's *Airbrush* and *Paintbrush* tools. The robe was painted after carefully masking off the edges of the shape and thus protecting the areas of the hands and face.

It is often easier to create separate layers for different elements of the painting. Here, for example, the character's right arm was painted all on its own layer, above the layer containing the painted robe.

10 Once the three separate figures were prepared in an almost-finished state – that is each on its own single flattened layer and in its own canvas – I simply dragged each figure into the main canvas by using the *Move* tool. With the earlier background sketch as a basis, I had built up a very simple 'set' to act as a backdrop for the characters, so I then positioned them within it.

The king had the uppermost layer so that he would appear in front of the others. The scale was also adjusted accordingly.

11 The apprentice wizard's magic spell was created in a separate layer in Photoshop, using the *FraxFlame* filter – one of the many Kai's Power Tools plug-ins that are available.

12 I was now ready to add the shadows. The background, visible here without the characters in position, reveals some of the construction. I wasn't concerned about the different elements not linking up tidily in areas where I knew the characters would be placed on top. The shadows cast by the characters were created using the *Airbrush* tool in *Multiply* mode, and were painted onto this background layer once I was sure of their final positions.

13 Everything finally comes together in the scene. While the individual components were still on separate layers, I used the *Airbrush* and *Eraser*, and the *Smudge* and *Blur* tools to blend everything together, remove any untidiness around the outlines of the figures and soften the edges in places to reduce any disjointedness between the figures and their background. The *Burn* tool was also useful for deepening shadows to help merge elements together. Contrast adjustments were made to the separate layers using *Image > Adjust > Brightness/Contrast.* And any colour discrepancies were corrected with

Image > Adjust > Color Balance. This helped guarantee that the characters looked correct together and in the same environment. Once I was happy that everything was working together effectively, I flattened the image and then went over it one last time, making small last-minute adjustments and tidying up any loose areas.

Rivendell

STEFFEN **S**OMMER, **AFTER FIVE YEARS** of art school at the Staedelschule in Frankfurt, Germany, and several years of experience as a traditional painter, discovered a passion for computer graphics. After working as a digital painter, 3D animator and production designer for several small companies in Germany, Steffen was fortunate enough to have his dream to work in cinema come true when he landed a job as a texture artist with PDI/DreamWorks in the USA, on the film *Shrek 2*.

Rivendell was the first major piece of 3D artwork that Steffen created, and it demonstrates some fundamental modelling techniques with 3ds max.

'Rivendell was done in my free time, using 3D Studio Max 2.5 and Fractal Design Painter. My passion for J.R.R. Tolkien's *The Lord of the Rings* trilogy, which had been the source of inspiration for many of my paintings and drawings as a child, was rekindled after many years when I heard about Peter Jackson's new film project. I immediately set about re-working one of the visions for

SOFTWARE 3DS MAX, PAINTER ARTIST STEFFEN SOMMER WEBSITE WWW.RAPH.COM EMAIL STEFFSOMMER@GMX.NET

Tolkien's Middle Earth that I'd created about 15 years earlier, as this design for Rivendell now didn't seem quite so viable in light of the forthcoming film project. As with every 3D work, I began by creating an extensive number of pencil studies, in order to explore my ideas for Rivendell as clearly as possible.

'I wanted from the outset to limit myself to just one part of the castle, and the still image shows the west wing of the outer wall. "My" Rivendell, due to the fissured mountains on which it sits, depicts a completely open structure, consisting of individual buildings connected by a series of bridges. In the background, the semi-circle of mountains that surround the castle is open to reveal a plain, allowing us a view of the Misty Mountains in the distance.'

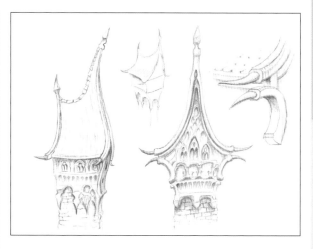

1 After developing the overall style of my Rivendell from the hundreds of drawings that I'd done, I then did a few more detailed pencil sketches of individual buildings. From these drawings, I tried to discover the best way of translating the design into a particular three-dimensional geometric form.

Rivendell consists almost exclusively of polygons. Only the roofs and trees are what are known as Patch Grids, a variant of NURBS surfaces in 3ds max. Good planning can save many hours of work when you come to modelling in 3D, so for this reason I spend a lot of time on the details at this early stage.

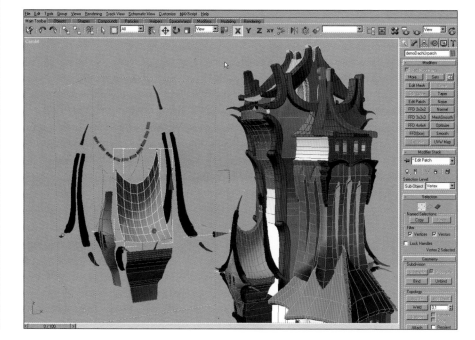

2 Rivendell is mostly modular in construction, and by re-using many of the parts, I can avoid a lot of extra work at both the texturing and modelling stages. When texturing, it was necessary to ensure that any repetitions were not visible. On the left of the screen is an exploded view to illustrate the construction process. All of the parts, except for the walls, are very simple geometrical patterns. The niches and windows within the walls are built up by way of Boolean operations and by using the edges of various polygons. Allocating the UV co-ordinates for the final texturing was particularly time-consuming at this stage.

3 With the exception of the lighting, the texturing stage took the most work to complete. Almost all of the textures are bitmaps created in Painter using a Wacom pad. These bitmaps are used for the *Diffuse*, *Specular* and *Bump* channels of simple Blinn Shaders – a mathematical shading model to represent convincing surface properties on otherwise smooth 3D geometry. I designed all of the ornaments, as I did with the overall architecture itself, using pencil and paper. Whilst I was very much influenced by Norman and Celtic art, I tried to find my own original versions à la *The Lord of the Rings*. Many of the textures were tileable, so that they could be re-used several times over. In the middle of the screen, you can see a *Bump* map in the *Shader Editor*, and the top-right window shows the *Diffuse* and *Bump* maps applied to the object and rendered in *Render View*.

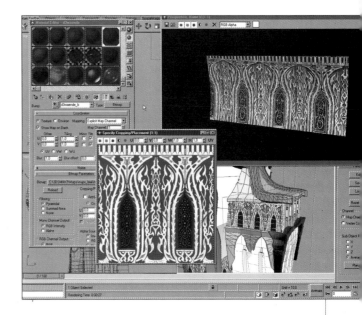

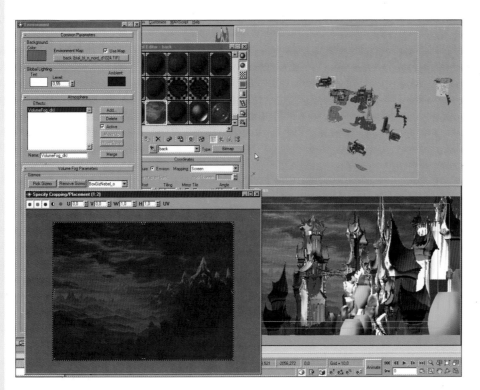

4 A deciding factor, as far as achieving a credible/realistic 3D image is concerned, is the portrayal of atmospheric conditions, such as the rays of light through fine water droplets, which give an impression of distance — in space, where there is no atmosphere, this is naturally not an issue. The yellow square at the top right of the screen shows 3ds max's *Fog Gizmo*, a helper *Object* that defines the position of the fog in the scene. On the left in the *Shader Editor*, you can see the painted background, which I did digitally using a Wacom drawing pad and Painter. I tried to avoid using photographic elements in order to retain the more naturally painted, fairytale look that I wanted for Middle Earth.

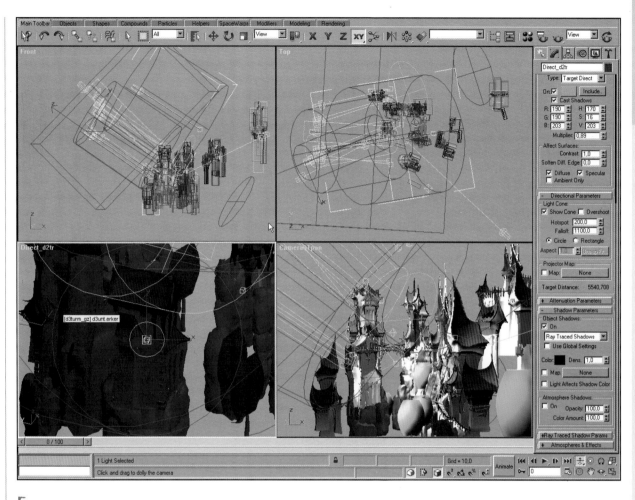

5 The last step — as I was not planning on having any animation for Rivendell — was the lighting. This is often a very time-consuming part of the process, as it always requires a lot of test rendering. In order to simulate the complex play of light in the real world, you often need dozens, sometimes even hundreds of lights for just one scene in the 3D environment.

For Rivendell, I wanted a dramatic lighting effect, as though the result of a cloudy sky that lets through only weak rays of sunlight. Clearly visible in the 3D view are the many 'direct lights' (which are the *Key* lights in this scene) simulating sunlight streaming in from the left. For fill lights there are two direct lights from top and bottom. In the top view, these can be seen from the bottom right. Both simulate the sunrays reflected off the sky and the surroundings. Some of the dark areas were lit with a few small spot-lights. The bottom left is a camera view through one of these lights. In the bottom right, you can see that the trees are designed from half-spheres, textured with *Diffuse, Bump*

and *Opacity* maps. The half-sphere has the advantage, unlike to flat sprites, that it enables rendering to the lit side. Sprites are flat surfaces, usually textured with an *Opacity* map, to create simple trees, bushes and so on in computer games. One disadvantage, however, is that the half-sphere only works from one particular camera angle.

Nowadays, I would probably build the trees out in full, as modern hardware can make light work of a few million polygons. My P2 266MHz computer had problems coping with 250,000

polygons, and my patience, while waiting for the rendering, quickly wore thin, too!

In my opinion, plant-simulating programs are still plagued by rendering mistakes and are unreliable, especially when it comes to shadow-casting.

For the lighting, I would ultimately hope to use global illumination rendering, although the rendering times for this very realistic lighting simulation are often so long that more traditional lighting techniques are still used widely in the film and effects industry.

Destination Future

SCIENCE FICTION ARTISTS HAVE RISEN TO THE CHALLENGE OF DEPICTING THE FUTURE WITH INCREASING SOPHISTICATION AND CREDIBILITY, EACH GENERATION OF ARTISTS SURPASSING ITS PREDECESSOR IN CREATING FANTASTIC, PROPHETIC VISIONS TO GRAB OUR ATTENTION WITH THE SHOCK OF THE NEW. THE INFLUENCE OF SCIENCE FICTION IMAGERY HAS BEEN SO PROFOUND THAT IT'S NOW UBIQUITOUS IN OUR CULTURE. IT PRESENTS US WITH INSPIRING VISIONS OF FUTURE TECHNOLOGIES AND WAYS OF LIFE, BUT ALSO WITH CONCEPTIONS OF THE CHILLINGLY PLAUSIBLE CONSEQUENCES OUR SCIENTIFIC PROGRESS COULD BRING.

3

MY OWN EARLY FORAYS INTO science fiction art began in near-infancy with my endless drawings of Daleks and Cybermen from *Doctor Who*. With the release of *Star Wars* and the tide of imitators that followed throughout the late 1970s, I was provided with an endless source of robots, spaceships and laser guns to reproduce and elaborate upon in my drawings. My enthusiasm was further fuelled by the discovery of science fiction comics like *Starlord* and then *2000AD*, in which the amazing work of Brian Bolland on *Judge Dredd* was especially inspirational.

The Victorian 'scientific romances' have been one of my great loves, and two of my favourites from among the inspiring artists of this early era of SF are Albert Robida and Warwick Goble. Robida was perhaps the first true science fiction artist, who in the 19th century envisaged a future of mechanized and chemical warfare.

Warwick Goble illustrated H.G.Wells's *The War of the Worlds* in *Pearson's Magazine*. His work has greater realism than the engravings that were more common at the time, as he was among the first to use paint techniques, rather than line, in print.

Another favourite early pioneer, in the pulp magazines of the 1930s, was Frank R. Paul. *Amazing Stories* was the first SF magazine, and Paul was its resident artist. His work

A classic Frank R. Paul cover painting for *Amazing Stories* in 1927, illustrating H.G. Wells' *The War of the Worlds*.

was so eye-catching, despite being a bit crude in execution, and his conceptual brilliance effectively defined the basic images of all subsequent science fiction.

A later innovator was Hubert Rogers, who by the 1940s had taken SF art to new levels of sophistication, moving away from the simplistic gadgetry and bug-eyed monsters of many of the splendidly lurid pulp covers of the era. Some of the true greats of SF and fantasy art followed, including the masterful Virgil Finlay and Hannes Bok, whose colour work was influenced by the dazzling transparent oil glazes seen in the paintings of Maxfield Parish.

Their contemporary Chesley Bonestell had a major influence on the public perception of SF, with artwork appearing on the cover of *Life* magazine in 1944 and concept work for George Pal's *Destination Moon*, igniting the SF movie boom of the 1950s. Their other collaborations included *When Worlds Collide* and *The War of the Worlds*.

THE SF BOOM

The 1950s saw an explosion of science fiction imagery. Everything from the optimism of Frank Hampson's *Dan Dare: Pilot of the Future* in *The Eagle*, which contained some of the most impressive artwork ever drawn for comics; to the depictions of mass destruction and widespread panic in 'B'-movie posters, later echoed in Norman B. Saunders' *Mars Attacks!* cards in the '60s.

Many of the artists whose work I enjoy first appeared in print in the 1970s, introducing a new era of modern SF art in the wake of *2001: A Space Odyssey*. One of the greats has been Chris Foss, whose paintings of streamlined spacecraft and robots, recalls the early inventions of Frank R. Paul, but rendered spectacular with realism.

A 1953 Virgil Finlay illustration for the Robert Sheckley story *Beside Still Waters*. Finlay's fine pen work made him the most popular artist in pulp magazines.

Above: **Stanley Meltzoff's** hugely influential painting for Robert Heinlein's *The Puppet Masters* appeared in 1952, and is widely considered to be a masterpiece of the sci-fi genre.

Right: **Sensational poster art for the Roger Corman film** *Not of this Earth*, **from 1956.**

The work of Jean Giraud, otherwise known as Moebius, has been a particular favourite of mine for many years. He is best known for his narrative artwork in *Metal Hurlant*, and his images often display an exotic palette, depicting the strangest of dreamlike technological environments. Among his accomplishments is costume design for *Alien*.

Conceptual design for films has produced some of the science fiction imagery that I find most inspirational. One of the most influential artists has been Ralph McQuarry with his visuals for the original *Star Wars* trilogy. The stylish artefacts designed by Syd Mead, as a conceptual futurist on many films (including *Alien* and *Blade Runner)*, pioneered the look of a gritty future of urban decay.

Another favourite of mine is Jim Burns. He has perfected his own style by highlighting not only the traditional elements of science fiction but also its organic and erotic overtones. He depicts land, sky and space vehicles in gleaming metal and plastic so perfectly that you can almost feel their cool metallic touch.

This kind of photo-realism in speculative industrial design prompts a natural progression to digital techniques. Science fiction more than any other fantasy genre can demand a level of 'finish' in the detailed representation of its imaginary worlds. Digital tools and techniques lend themselves extremely well to this, and futuristic hardware and environments can now be rendered with increasing levels of realism and credibility.

Imperial Freighter and Droid

PAUL TOPOLOS STUDIED FINE ART in Britain and the USA. He worked several years with the Lucas companies, first at LucasArts as a storyboard artist, concept designer, 3D background artist, texture painter, lead artist and art director. At Lucasfilm Entertainment he worked briefly as a storyboard artist on *Star Wars Episode I* and as a matte painter for the previsualization crew on *Episode II*. Currently he is a digital matte painter at Pixar Animation Studios.

Paul demonstrates his techniques in the creation of two rapid production paintings, using Photoshop to combine the application of digital paint with photographic elements, to define the look of hardware and environments. Here he takes us through the creation of paintings of a spacecraft and a droid, for the *Star Wars Rebel Strike* game.

'When I was a child, I liked to draw. My father repaired copy machines for a living, so there was always a lot of paper lying around the house. Although I really enjoyed it, I could be very cautious and highly strung about drawing, especially when using ink pens. Nothing has changed for me as an adult. When working in pencil, charcoal, Photoshop or any other medium that is malleable and correctable, I can feel good, enjoy life, and sometimes even draw and paint boldly. But when it came time for me as an adult to do conceptual design, the preferable style at the time was only ink markers. Peter Chan at LucasArts was a

SOFTWARE **PHOTOSHOP** ARTIST **PAUL TOPOLOS** EMAIL **PTOPOLOS@PIXAR.COM**

master, and it was intimidating to watch him work. Much like Doug Chiang, Peter could work up a drawing first using lighter shades of markers until the mass was built up, then without a care in the world he would draw in dark ink lines and add accents of painted white gouache. I had never studied industrial design, and had no experience with markers. When I attempted something like that, I would feel like a 10-year-old again who had just ruined the Tie Fighter drawing he'd spent hours on. I realized I was someone who had to be able to change and adapt his work as it progressed, and even after it was done.

'I tried to do concept drawings just in pencil, but that was not as well received as marker drawings. I feared I would never get a chance to do concept design again. It was strange for me as an artist, because my storyboards, figure drawings, 3D backgrounds and Photoshop work were not bad. I had a reputation for working quickly and well, with a consistent style that most people liked. It wasn't until I went to work as a matte painter for the previsualization team at Skywalker Ranch for *Star Wars Episode II* that I saw a good way to do conceptual design. Working in the art department side of the building, I was able to watch how both Ryan Church and Erik Tiemens worked. I saw that they were doing production paintings in Painter and Photoshop. They would start with a file that would begin as their under drawing and be worked up into their final. Everything could be tweaked, and it seemed like nothing could be ruined. This felt like something new and exciting in conceptual design.

'At the same time as I was working at Lucasfilm as a matte painter, I was art directing *Star Wars* games for LucasArts at a company called Factor Five. I had to do the conceptual designs for the upcoming game, and decided to use what I had learned from Erik and Ryan'.

IMPERIAL FREIGHTER

There was going to be an Imperial Freighter in the game *Rogue Squadron III: Rebel Strike*. From a design side, I knew that Imperial ships were utilitarian, cold and somewhat simple and brutal in design. They would be mass-produced, and a freighter would need to be big, bulky and not exactly pretty. Doug Chiang had always talked about how a design needs to read well the first time you see it. In an instant, you need to see whether something is good or bad, dangerous or weak, and so on. He also talked of the importance of a design working as a silhouette and being able to tell the directionality of a vehicle from any angle. I knew that a freighter would not be sleek or stylish, and yet I needed to convey the idea that it was a bad ship belonging to the enemy. I decided to go with aggressive, angry angles, and a shape that was reminiscent of several things: the bulky sandcrawler from *Episode IV*, a 1930s airship and a pig. Doug was always big on including shapes that feel familiar to an audience.

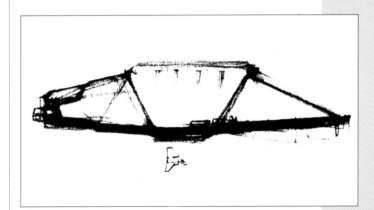

1 I began with a pencil sketch I had done a long time ago which was loosely based on something I'd seen in a Ralph McQuarrie drawing. I had saved it and the idea had always felt 'Star Warsy' to me, with its big, simple shapes and tiny details. I added to it, and it felt like I was going on the right track.

3

2 I made several quick greyscale designs in Photoshop, that were based on the brainstorming that I was doing, and I showed these to my boss. I would use the *Lasso* tool to make selections of the shapes that I wanted and dump *Paint Buckets* into them. The windows were cut out of Coruscant buildings that I had made for *Episode II* and the engines were quickly blocked-in by painting in a *Color Dodge* layer. The final image would be painted directly on top of what I started in my initial concept.

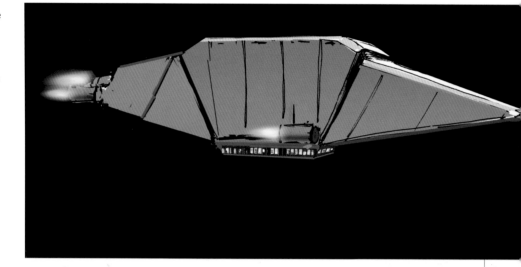

3 Once the design was signed off, I began the process of refining and strengthening the shapes. I used the *Lasso* tool to redefine the basic shapes and the *Line* tool to begin the detailing process. The *Burn* tool, along with overlaying metallic photographs, can help in the ageing process.

Lighting becomes an important issue early on. The freighter is mainly backlit with secondary light coming from the tiny but powerful engines and the cargo bay. Windows help with scale, as do the two AT-AT Walkers coming out with troops. The Walker itself was a render from the game that

I cut out and scaled down. I wanted to put the freighter within a landscape and found a photograph and began manipulating it towards a more dramatic time of day. I used *Curves* to darken it and make it more contrasting. I pushed the colour towards purple-blue and

painted on top of it to add more mountains, clouds and a setting sun. Using the *Circular Gradient* tool, I was able to get the glow of the sunset, and by *Motion Blurring* a line at the horizon and then setting the layer on *Color Dodge,* I got a nice glow from the sun onto the landscape.

4 I tend to work sloppily and all over the place at once. One moment I'm making colour balance choices, the next I'll lay down perspective lines on a separate layer to make sure things are lining up, and then quickly put in a bit of detail with ill-aimed brush strokes and hope to clean it up later. I'm not recommending it as a way to work, and in many ways it feels like a dumb way to paint, but it's what I know and somehow fits into the way I think.

As I pressed on with the design, I realized that there could also be a ramp at the back of the ship and a tiny cockpit near the nose. My earlier shape seemed too simple and didn't give enough sense of scale, so I added slight height variations at the top, along with small rows of windows and lights. *Star Wars* ships,

especially Imperial ones, tend to have big, plain metal plating with tiny detail bits and lines to help create scale. I added slanted lines that echoed other shapes and made the rear engines stronger. I also quickly roughed-in panel details to see how they fit in with the rest. Since there was room in the composition, and I hadn't really thought about composition anyway, I put in another freighter and its Tie Fighter escort to show how the little engines would rotate to a horizontal position when flying away.

I was beginning to enjoy the idea of this big clunky ship with these really tiny engines that keep it afloat. Its physics were a little unreal, but I liked the idea that the technology was so advanced that it was possible to fly, like the tiny engines that propel an airship.

5 The finishing tweaks and smoothing of surfaces happen. A little more light hitting on the ground near the sunset, a shadow from a second Walker coming out of the bay, and glints of reflective light on the AT-AT legs help add finish. The original purpose of the painting was just to give something for the modeller to use

as reference to build a 3D model. It was not meant for any specific shot but rather to help sell the idea of the design by giving it a little mood. Using Photoshop, it didn't take much extra time to put in the background, colour, lighting and other vehicles, and all of it helps convey a story, and a sense of time, place and theme.

DROID

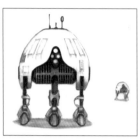

1 I had a drawing of an R2-D2-like droid from years back, which I thought I could use for the *Rebel*

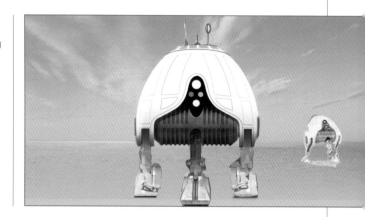

Strike game. In the end, it didn't get used, but I had enjoyed doing the picture, so I tucked it away. I took the pencil drawing and scanned it in.

In hindsight, I believe it's better to start fresh on the computer. I found myself fighting against the drawing in the beginning and ultimately just covered the whole thing up with digital paint and lines.

3 I tend to first work a design into a clean shape with simple detail and then dirty it up a bit later. In this case, I had chosen a rather boring front-on view of the droid – the reason being that it allowed me the quick luxury of cleaning and delineating one side and then flipping that half over to get the whole droid perfect. With the general shape cleaned up, I can really see what is working or not in the design and hopefully make any changes before I add the paint job and the detail. The ageing and paint will always make something look better and feel more real, but it's good to have a solid design working for you before you start to add the dressing. It's easy for me to use my model painting experience as a crutch to make a bad design look better just because it's painted. By this stage, I had decided to change the background to look more appropriate, using part of a production still from Tunisia for the ground and a different sky that had converging lines towards the centre.

2 I realized that the original legs were too long and that the feet were not really an appropriate design for an R2 droid. It needed some more recognizable shapes, so I cropped off the legs from a reference photograph of an R2 unit from *Episode I* and pasted them into my droid. I blocked-out the major shapes of the body, using the *Ellipse* tool to approximate the curves from my drawing, and dumped a *Paint Bucket* of what I wanted the local colour to be. I *Stroked* ellipses to get the panel lines that you see in droids and cut out lights and lenses that I had in my own texture library.

The model-makers at ILM have large inventories of bits and pieces from plastic model kits, and I try to keep a similar digital library of pod racing engine parts, photographs of *Star Wars* models, and cockpit lights to cut and paste into my *Star Wars* images. It's a habit from my days in digital model painting, and I find it can help add a little extra bit of realism in concept work, or it can at least spark some inspiration to what mechanical bits look like.

To provide a background, I placed the droid against a simple desert landscape and sky photograph. Again, in hindsight, this was probably a bit too easy to do. It's very good to paint in a sky and clouds of your own, because you can better control exactly what you want it to look like, but it is very cheap and easy to throw in a photograph of something and see whether or not the idea sticks.

3

4 From a pristine image, I begin to beat it up and give it some history. There is always a sense of 'pre-life' with every *Star Wars* character, ship or object, and I wanted to show that within the concept. For ageing, I use the *Airbrush* tool set on *Dissolve* at a low *Opacity* and brush in a dark or rusty colour. I paint into areas of heavy use or where two surfaces meet. *Motion Blurring* on these *Dissolved* pixels in the direction of gravity, or in line with any stains, created movement by about 30 pixels or so to produce a nice streaky stain and the feeling of use or movement. This can work well for speed stains on anything that moves fast. Using the *Dissolve* setting and doing a *Gaussian Blur* can make realistic effects of grime and rust without directionality. I use photographs of metal that I cut and overlay over certain surfaces. I sometimes *Erase* sections of the metal to avoid a busy feel. Varying the material properties within the droid is important to give a sense of richness to the parts. Within the droid, there will be different types of metals and plastics, all of which react differently to light and have a unique look. The body has a different material quality than the parts that are in constant movement or that are in direct contact with the ground. I also began to try and give a little life to the lights within the face of the droid by setting glows on *Color Dodge* within a layer.

5 Now comes the detailing and colour. I'd received some criticism about the lack of functionality with the droid. People wanted to know what it could do. I began to expose some panels and show that, like R2-D2, this droid had mechanical arms and outlets and plugs that could do multiple tasks. There also needed to be a colour scheme. The precedent had been set that any Rebel or 'good guy' design tended to be an earth tone colour, so I gave him red stripes with the paint peeling off. I bleached out some of the colour using the *Dodge* tool and dirtied up other colour using the *Burn* tool. I messed up the edges with an oddly shaped brush in the local colour of the off-white droid. Then I turned my attention to improving the setting for the model. I put in reflective light from the sand and little specular glints. It seemed logical to me to put a moisture evaporator in the distance. By warming up the sand, I made the background feel a lot hotter, dustier and desert-like. I also blurred it out a bit so that it looked less like a photograph and more like an appropriate setting.

Dredd Gang

FRAZER IRVING STARTED WORKING professionally four years ago with *2000AD*. His first proper assignment was a dark, Lovecraftian tale called *The Necronauts,* which is now collected as a book from publishers Rebellion. He moved swiftly onto a variety of different strips for *2000AD*, from retina-searing psychedelic superheroes to high contrast vampire horror to heavy brooding painted drama. Also during this period he drew books for the American market, such as the fictionalized adventures of Charles Fort in *Fort: Prophet of the Unexplained* from Dark Horse Comics (also available as a collected edition) and *The Authority: Scorched Earth* for DC Comics. He is currently doing many illustrations for Wizards of the Coast products and is still working on various strips for *2000AD*, for which he produced this cover image. For this depiction of a group of famous *Judge Dredd* villains, Frazer used Photoshop to create line work with colour, combining traditional and digital media.

'This image was commissioned by Andy Diggle, then editor of *2000AD* during summer 2002. The brief was very simple, as all I had to do was create an image which illustrated a scene from the *Judge Dredd* story contained within. The story involved a group of Dredd's old enemies travelling through time to gain revenge on him, and the cover for this episode was set aside for the chapter where the villains appear for the first time.

'With this restriction in place, it was relatively simple to arrange the image, since all it had to be was a group shot of a bunch of bad guys. So my first task was to design a composition that showed each of them clearly, allowed for logos and type, and was dramatic enough to capture the essence of the strip.'

SOFTWARE PHOTOSHOP ARTIST FRAZER IRVING WEBSITE WWW.FRAZERIRVING.COM EMAIL ART@FRAZERIRVING.COM

3

2 This was a drawing traced from the original pencil sketch using a marker pen. I did this to define the details of the characters and the set up the lighting. I already had the idea that there would be a sort of 'mist' clouding the feet of the guys, as well as spooky light from below and some cosmic background, all of which made it to the final image.

1 These pencil sketches were first drawn on paper at print size to explore a few different compositions that I had in mind.

Because I was working in Mac OS 9 at this point, on a G4 with only 640MB of RAM, I didn't feel comfortable attempting to draw the sketches directly into Photoshop, so at this point all of my doodles were drawn naturally and scanned in. The sketches were all pretty similar, the main difference being the focal point.

In the end we chose the shot with the Monkey guy at the front bottom, as it resonated far better with the idea that these hoodlums had just popped out of some dimensional gateway.

3 The next stage was to draw the images. Having scanned in the marker pen sketch and resized it to fit the proper art board dimensions, I printed this guide out on A3 paper and took it to a light box. Here I traced the rough images to Bristol board individually so that I could composite them separately in Photoshop. One suggestion made by the editor was to have the *2000AD* logo placed between the mid-ground figures, to create a sense of depth, and so therefore I had the mission to create a final document that would have each character floating on his own layer. These traced images were inked using a Windsor and Newton series 7 number 1 sable brush, and then they were scanned-in as individual greyscale files.

3

4 The next stage was to create a master document. I opened a pre-sized cover template in greyscale and pasted in the marker pen sketch for placement. Then I copied and pasted in each of the other figures (after first cleaning up any stray lines and blemishes) as rough cut outs, using the *Transform* tool to size them to fit the layout. Once each figure was in place, I simply erased the marker pen guide and was left with a document with each figure on his own layer, in the correct order.

5 Next I needed to get each figure *Transformed* into a line layer. Since they were all pasted as cut-outs with black and solid white, I needed to isolate the black. To do that, I copied each of the figures individually and pasted them into a new layer in *Quick Mask* mode. Then I converted this mask back to selection and *Inverted* it, giving me the black lines only as a selection. Then it was a simple matter of filling the selection with black and setting the layer to *Preserve Transparency*, and my line layer was complete.

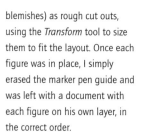

6 Once I had all my figures as line layers, I deleted the original figures.

Then I set up a new layer directly beneath each of the figures and linked each new layer to its parent figure. On this new layer, I used the *Pencil* tool to paint in a flat colour, in this case green, to act as the base for the colour work on each figure. Each of the figures needed to be painted in full, and the background figures needed some extra areas filled in to cover the gaps behind the group.

Once each figure was painted in with flat colour, and the edges tidied up to remove any rough parts, the colour layers were set to *Preserve Transparency* and a flat green was filled in the background layer.

7 Next was the painting: I moved to the *Paintbrush* tool and used the default brushes from Photoshop to start painting in the tones. As you can see, it really was a simple matter of painting on light, as the flat green provided the mid-tones and the lines provided the black.

8 Once I had painted the tones on each figure; I decided to create space. To do this I did two things: firstly I changed the colours. Using the *Hue/Saturation* tool, I explored the colour schemes that I felt would work. Having chosen green as my base colour, I figured the best way to bring figures forward from that would be to alter their temperature. This led me to choose a warm ochre for the foreground, getting slowly cooler as they recede. Staying with

monochrome was important so as not to make the image confusing. It's a very simple and direct idea, and additional colours would have ruined this effect.

The second thing I did was to paint a green onto the line layers. I set the line layers to *Preserve Transparency* and used the *Brush* tool to wash colour gently onto the black lines. With the figures at the back, I used the *Gradient* tool to ensure there was an even mist where the black lines met the green *Fill* behind them.

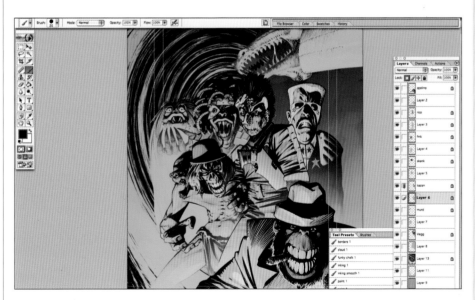

9 The final stage was creating the background.

I needed a cosmic effect for the portal, so I simply took a scan of some paint splashes, converted it to black and white and then used the *Distort* filters and the *Contrast* tool to distort it enough to suit my needs. Overall, I believe that this image was a

harmonious mix of traditional and digital media. This is the method that I immediately use when required to produce line work with colour.

Air Combat

RYAN CHURCH'S CLIENTS and employers include Walt Disney Imagineering, Universal Studios, Industrial Light and Magic, and Lucasfilm. Ryan is currently Concept Design Supervisor for *Star Wars Episode III* and a Senior Art Director at ILM, where his roles include designing and illustrating vehicles, droids, architectures and environments and art directing final shots and assets.

Here Ryan demonstrates his very fluid approach to digital painting techniques, using translucent washes within Corel Painter.

'One of the many advantages of digital media is that even the smallest sketch can be brought up to a final illustration. I keep a "digital sketchbook" of low-resolution sketches which I like to do when my imagination is feeling fertile. I work small and quick so that I can get out the most ideas with the least amount of effort and planning. When I find some time to explore a sketch as a rendering, I simply copy it and increase the resolution. By lowering the contrast, I can then sketch back over it, tightening it up with each iteration. At that point in the design, the gesture and silhouette are more important than the details or even the colour.'

SOFTWARE **PAINTER** ARTIST **RYAN CHURCH** WEBSITE **WWW.RYANCHURCH.COM** EMAIL **RYANCHURCH@EARTHLINK.NET**

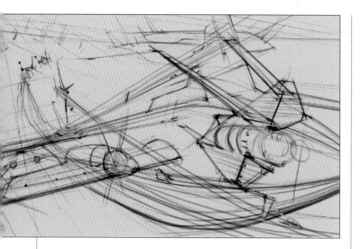

1 A painting like this will start with a loose black-and-white value composition that answers all of the basic questions and establishes the 2D relationships of elements on the page.

This is really the fun part, when you take your design sketches and work from them to form a 2D image that is reasonably accurate in design, perspective, action and composition.

3 To start the final painting, I block-in colour and tone with translucent media, which allows me to preserve my line work for as long as possible. At a certain point, I will switch to opaque media and tighten up the illustration for as long as my time

is budgeted. I like to work across the whole frame and to keep the detail level constantly consistent throughout it. This means that I can literally walk away from it at any time and still have a painting that is, if not 'finished', at least a 'cohesive' work.

2 From there, I will create a tight line drawing that helps me nail down the designs more accurately. Here I check

my perspective, tighten up the design and create the template from which my painting will come.

4 The eye is drawn to the right-hand side, where the large, dark shape of the foreground craft contrasts with the light of the background. Sharing the foreground is another craft, pursued by the first, and itself

chasing three more rocket planes. Smoke and condensation trails lead the eye from right to left.

Large mid-ground airships reinforce this right-to-left view and help establish both a sense of depth and speed.

Skull Syker

KARL RICHARDSON has risen to prominence in recent years by producing some of the most striking comic-strip and cover artwork for Games Workshop's *Warhammer* and *Warhammer 40,000*. For The Black Library's *Warhammer Monthly*, he has also drawn *Daemonifuge 2*, *Lone Wolves* and the *Eye of Terror* story, *Last Stand on Yayor*, as well as numerous cover paintings. He has also had work producing covers for *Inferno!* magazine. Karl is currently working on the *Judge Dredd* strip, for *2000AD*.

In Karl's step-by-step workthrough, he reveals some of his painting methods using Photoshop, and creates a detailed design concept for one of his own *Tankskulls* comic-book characters, Skull Syker.

'Although I've always loved science fiction and fantasy art and have been drawing since I can remember, it wasn't until I was into my late 20s that I decided to have a serious go at it myself. I'd attempted a few acrylic paintings, but never had the patience to finish them. They were a radical departure from my regular cartoon work in style, and especially in the fact that I could envisage, sketch and complete a cartoon in a matter of hours – whereas it could take me days to get even half way through a painting.

'I was then introduced to a computer, and more importantly Photoshop, by an artist friend. To say it was life-changing would be a bit dramatic, but it was a moment of enlightenment that would change the fortunes of my career considerably. Working with Photoshop enabled me to speed up dramatically, and without the mess. It also gave me the confidence to try things that I would've hesitated to with a traditional painting. Within a couple of months, I was able to approach Games Workshop with digital art, and since then they've kept me pretty busy doing numerous covers and comic strip work. Whenever I get any spare time, I indulge in my own project called *Tankskulls* which, once I've finished designing everything, I hope to get published in the not too distant future.'

SOFTWARE **PHOTOSHOP** ARTIST **KARL RICHARDSON** WEBSITE **WWW.MACHINE-PUNK.COM** EMAIL **KARL.RICHARDSON24@NTLWORLD.COM**

1 Photoshop is pretty memory-intensive, so I've got a PC with a 2.5GHz processor and a whopping 1 gigabyte of RAM. I start by scanning the pencil sketch in greyscale at 600dpi, so that it's nice and big. Once it's in Photoshop, I then change from greyscale mode into RGB. Published work is always printed in CMYK, but while I'm working on an image, I prefer it to be RGB because that makes for a considerably smaller file than one in CMYK, and this really counts when you're working on an image of 150MB with 10 layers. Once I've finished the image, I'll then convert it to CMYK. If there's a noticeable change in colour, then I'll just use Photoshop's *Color Balance* and *Hue/Saturation* tools to correct it. But at this stage all that still lies ahead.

2 I didn't go to art college, so when it comes to painting I don't have any formal training, and perhaps this is why there's little structure to the way that I approach my work. I've never read books about art technique, preferring to be inspired by the Frazettas and Bisleys of this world. If I *had* gone to art college or read more on the subject, perhaps my progress would have been quicker, but I think by experimenting and through trial and error, some of the most important lessons are learned.

I usually start by blocking-in the character with a relatively dark shade of the colour that I believe I'll end up with, painted at medium *Opacity* on a new layer. In this case, Skull Syker is mainly a green-grey metal colour, even his flesh. I go as dark as I can while still being able to see the line art underneath.

3 At the start, I'm quite tentative, even working digitally. It takes me about 20 minutes to warm up properly, so I normally begin on a part of the picture that doesn't include any vitally important details (avoiding the face as yet). In this case, I start with Skull Syker's chest plate and arm, adding detail in a lighter value using the *Airbrush*, applied on a new layer. After that, I also tentatively add a bit of highlighting to his helmet in exactly the same way.

The head is obviously an important part of the picture, and if I don't get it right it can undermine any good work I achieve elsewhere in the picture. Once I'm warmed-up and feeling confident, I like to get enough of the face or head done to satisfy me. If I'm happy with the head, it sets me up for the rest of the painting.

4 As you can see, I'm now gradually working across his torso. I tend to work up some areas with quite a bit of detail, even with high- and lowlights, while other areas haven't even been touched. This is mostly to do with my lack of patience and wanting to see a finished area with which I'm pleased, in order for me to move on to another area. Of course, there's no obvious light source in this painting because it's a concept piece, so I've simply decided the light is going to come from the left. Still using the *Airbrush*; I'm adding pale blue lowlights to add more interest and a general three-dimensional look.

5 At this stage you might notice I've started to add some textures to Syker, especially on the left weapon. I took a photo of a section of wall in my garden and scanned it in. I then copied the background layer of the photo and *Multiplied* it. It's now just a case of selecting, with one of the *Lasso* tools, the desired sections of this layer and dragging them across to the chosen parts of the artwork. I could turn down the *Opacity* or use the *Eraser* to get rid of any unwanted bits. This helps to blend the textured layer so that I could get the effect I wanted.

I actually have mixed feelings about these sorts of methods, because it feels like I'm cheating; but as long as I don't overdo it, and remember that textures and filters don't make a painting but simply embellish what is already a good, solid piece of work, I'll be fine. Good drawing and composition are paramount to a great painting.

Not all of my digital paintings contain textures, and in fact one of my favourite pieces, *Lone Wolves*, doesn't contain a single texture or filter effect at all. I just used the default brushes available in Photoshop.

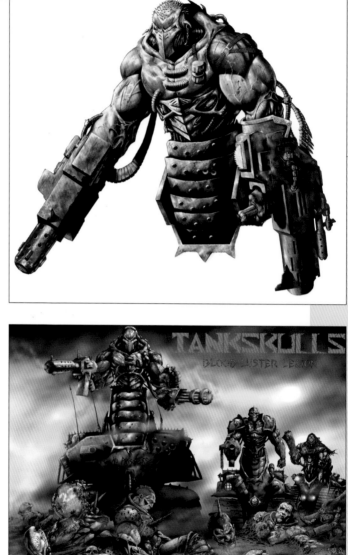

6 I'm in sight of the finishing line now, and it's really just a case of adding all of the final touches like bullet holes, studs, rivets and more blood. In the case of details like bullet holes, I usually make a new file and paint these details separately, then drag them into the picture. This way, I can have numerous bullet holes when actually I've only painted one. The same applies to studs and rivets, etc. However, I normally modify the odd one with *Airbrush* or *Paintbrush* to give the illusion that they're all unique.

Similarly icons, like one on Skull Syker's machine gun, are rendered separately and dragged in. By going to *Edit > Transform*, then either *Perspective*, *Distort* or *Skew*, I can modify the icon's shape to get the correct perspective. Although this doesn't really apply to a stand-alone painting, it's invaluable for saving time when doing comic strip work, when I might have to draw the same iconography literally hundreds of times.

By this time, I can be working on 10 or 15 different layers, bloodstains on one layer, icons on another. The image may well be 150MB by now, but it's not until I'm totally happy with it that I can begin to *Merge* any layers or *Flatten* them entirely.

7 Well, I've got my Skull Syker bust fully completed now, so I'll no doubt be referring to this image countless times as I work with the character in any future comic strips. I wouldn't be surprised if this artwork turned up in a full-blown painting in the near future, as part of the ongoing *Tankskulls* project.

Ape vs. Robot

ROBERTO CAMPUS IS ORIGINALLY from Italy but now lives near Boston, Massachusetts, in the USA. He is a professional freelance illustrator and comic-book colourist, and *Thundercats* and *The Hulk* are among his most recently published comic book titles. He has also worked on computer games, book covers and role-playing games. His favourite subjects are fantasy and science fiction, and his style ranges from anime to ultra-realistic.

'My introduction to computer graphics was the film *Tron*. I was simply awestruck by it. I consider it a milestone in the timeline of digital visuals, as it was the first movie to make such heavy use of 3D graphics. Home computers were still in their infancy in the early 1980s, and the options were limited, but after *Tron*, I knew that the digital medium would evolve to one day compete against traditional media. Shortly thereafter, when I was about 12, I was already creating computer graphics using programs that I wrote myself in BASIC language. The best you could get back then was a very low-resolution image with maybe 16 colours, but it was still fascinating to me because of its promise of unrivalled possibilities.

'Today, thanks to the rapid advances in computer graphics technology, we are finally seeing digital art empowering both young and old generations of artists with a new creative tool. It is a tool that, in some ways, is not yet fully appreciated, as some people assume – quite wrongly – that the computer is creating the artwork, rather than the artist himself.

'Fortunately, as more people learn that digital tools are just another way of expressing the boundless creativity of an artist, we professionals in the field can enjoy more recognition and respect. I see artists, who once only utilized traditional media, embracing digital art when they realize that it can provide them with faster production times. Also, I see 3D computer graphics as the area in

SOFTWARE **PAINTER, PHOTOSHOP** ARTIST **ROBERTO CAMPUS** WEBSITE **WWW.ROBERTOCAMPUS.COM** EMAIL **BOB@ROBERTOCAMPUS.COM**

which most of the evolution is taking place right now. It won't be long before we see fully convincing human characters – indistinguishable from real human actors – on a film screen. Setting aside the need (or lack thereof) for virtual actors, that will be the point when I think we can say that digital art finally reached maturity.'

In this tutorial, Roberto demonstrates his painting techniques, using a combination of tools available within Painter and Photoshop.

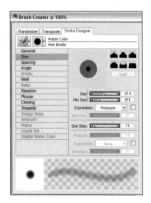

1 This illustration was done for a trading card game. I was required to paint a fight between a cybernetic ape and a robot (not a modern-looking one, but one closer to those from the old science fiction B-movies of the 1950s). This sketch was done using the *Brushes* tool in Painter and a Wacom tablet.

Usually, I try to sketch as fast as I can, concentrating only on shapes, light and shadow, pose and action. One factor to consider during the sketching process is that if you stop too often to think, rationalize or analyze what you are sketching from your imagination, then you may interfere with your right hemisphere while it is hard at work, attempting to translate the image in your mind's eye to your hand and then the paper/screen. See it as the same kind of process that goes on in your mind when you hear a word: you instantly know the meaning, right? But if you stop and repeat the word over and over, it may start to sound weird and to lose its connection to the concept linked to it. I think the same theory applies to the sketching process. Just let it flow.

2 This is the main stage of the artwork, where I paint in the foreground elements. Still using Painter's *Brushes* tool and a medium *Opacity* setting, I concentrate on reshaping all of the forms to their final position and dimensions. I also do some work on the lighting. At this point, I may use reference pictures for refining the way that the light and shadow would play on the various parts of the subjects. The robot was done completely from imagination. It consists of simple shapes and, as such, it was not too difficult to imagine how it would react to the light sources. Notice the yellow highlights added at this stage; I was already planning to add the electric sparks later on.

During this part of the process, I used brushes of various sizes, with smaller and more carefully positioned strokes.

3 At this point, I imported the image into Photoshop. Using the *Smudge* tool (with very low *Opacity*), I blended the brush strokes on the robot to give it a smoother metallic look. Then, I used the *Dodge* tool to add highlights to some areas that were still too dark, especially on the monkey's arms and head and also on the robot's right arm. I find the *Dodge* tool very useful to get highlights in place quickly. This technique is especially handy because time is a rare commodity for the commercial illustrator, especially when working on multiple projects. I then moved to add a bit more detail on the monkey's fur by using the *Smudge* tool with a small brush. The *Smudge* tool is extremely helpful when working on hair, fur or any other flowing curved shapes, especially if you have a pressure-sensitive tablet and stylus. The background was then added using the regular *Paintbrush* tool with a medium *Opacity* and 0% hardness brush.

3

4 Now that the painting was finished, I moved on to adding all of the various effects. The first step was to add some electric sparks. I simply painted them on a separate layer and then applied an *Outer Glow* effect.

I then moved on to softening the brighter areas of the image (this is an effect that I usually add to all of my artwork). The process goes as follows: first, I flattened the image into a single layer called 'art'. This 'art' layer was then duplicated to form a new layer, which I called 'glow'. Next, I applied a *Gaussian Blur* filter with a large radius setting to the 'glow' layer, thus achieving a very blurred image. Then I set the blending mode of the 'glow' layer to *Lighten* and lowered its *Opacity* down to 20%. Now, with the original layer showing through, the image highlights look a lot softer and more natural. Finally, I flattened the image again and adjusted its *Brightness* and *Luminosity* settings using the *Levels* tool.

As a finishing touch, my signature logo was added. It is drawn large because the artwork would be very small on the trading card, and I wanted the logo to be still seen clearly.

Tank Mech

FRED GAMBINO HAS WORKED AS AN illustrator for more than 20 years, originally using traditional media such as acrylics and oils. His client list includes nearly all the major publishers on both sides of the Atlantic, major advertising agencies, and more recently DNA in Dallas, Texas, for whom he did concept work for the Oscar-nominated film *Jimmy Neutron: Boy Genius*. Fred has since worked on a children's TV series, designing everything from costumes to environments to vehicles, and is currently busy with further top-secret film work, about which he can reveal nothing at the moment.

In this step-by-step, Fred demonstrates his techniques involving photographic elements refined and manipulated in Photoshop, and working in unison with composited artefacts modelled in 3D using LightWave.

'About eight years ago, seeing the writing on the wall and fearing that I was going to be left behind, I went out and spent a small fortune on a Mac, printer, scanner and software, equipment that seems ludicrously under-powered and expensive by today's standards. This was a huge leap of faith, since prior to my actually buying all this stuff I didn't know the difference between RAM and my right elbow. I piled the boxes in my room and with a sinking feeling realized that I had only the vaguest notion of how to put it together.

'Despite that, this was a good career move on my part: I took to working in the virtual realm like a duck to water, and rather than being left behind, I was one of the first to produce the kind of work that I was doing digitally, particularly in the British publishing industry. This "new" look stood me in good stead, although initially there was

---

SOFTWARE **LIGHTWAVE, PHOTOSHOP,** ARTIST **FRED GAMBINO** WEBSITE **WWW.FREDGAMBINO.CO.UK** EMAIL **FREDGAMB@GLOBALNET.CO.UK**

something of a mountain to climb with traditional art directors who were not yet ready to receive work that was submitted on disc.

'My work is now almost exclusively realized digitally the "new" look no longer applies, but I just enjoy the process of working digitally much more than working traditionally. However, in principle, the working practices detailed below, at least as far as gathering and producing the necessary reference materials goes, differ very little from my pre-computer days. The main difference is that then I would create my space ships as physical models, built out of found objects and cannibalized model kits, whereas now they are created in the computer and, of course, I no longer spend hours or days working up a square inch of acrylic painting to a desired finish, a process I can live without. There may come a time in the future when I am driven to pick up a paintbrush again, but for now I have lost any desire to work that way, unless specifically commissioned to do so.'

TANK MECH

This image is one of a number produced for Penguin Putnam in New York for the *Battletech* series, based on the successful role-playing game of the same name. Sometimes I get a manuscript to read, sometimes a short synopsis. Usually with this client I get a brief describing the scene and a description of how the figures are supposed to look.

Since these books relate to the *Battletech* game, the machines are already designed, and I generally get a line drawing of the machine in question. In that sense, this series is atypical of what I normally have to do, as the whole process of conceptualizing the hardware has been removed, although it is still up to me to determine colour and markings.

1 My normal practice in this early stage is to sit down at the drawing board and scribble a number of thumbnail sketches. Once I have a composition that I like, I scan the sketch, which is sometimes only an inch or so square, into the computer. This retains all those spontaneous lines and squiggles that come straight from the subconscious and add so much to the feel of a piece. I'll then blow it up to the finished size, going on to colour the rough using Photoshop. Sometimes when figures are involved, I'll use Poser to help me nail down the pose and start making lighting decisions.

2 Once the rough is approved, I move into the photographic studio. Occasionally my dining room cleared of furniture doubles as a studio if the shot can be achieved in that restricted space. With this shot, I needed something larger in order to be able to get back far enough and low enough from the characters.

The low angle point of view determined in the rough really required putting the models up on a platform. It's easy to get carried away with dramatic angles when designing on the computer, but it can sometimes lead to difficulties when trying to re-create that in the real world. I have a good relationship with a local photographer from whom I used to rent office space, so I'm lucky in having access to this kind of facility. At this point, I need to dress the models in something approximating the visual.

Over the years, I have accumulated a large collection of useful clothing and can generally cobble together something that's close to the image that I have in mind. For the Battletech series, the local army store has also proved invaluable. In these days of Photoshop and its associated digital trickery, it's a lot easier to manipulate these rough approximations into the desired effect. With this image, however, since the characters were described as civilians in battered clothing, I could pretty well use what I had to hand. I also gave them props to stand in for the weapons that they'd be holding, made, with no expense spared, from postage tubes and toy guns.

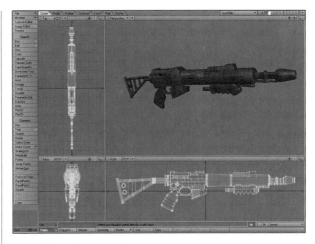

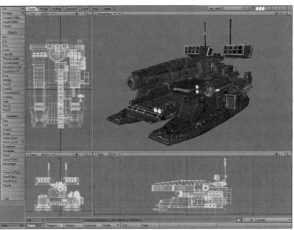

3 The next stage is to create any hardware and/or any backgrounds that will be required for the image. I like to model and texture the majority of these elements in 3D. My preferred 3D software at the moment is LightWave. I started with Alias Sketch (which has now morphed into Maya) followed by Electric Image. I now almost exclusively use LightWave and like it mainly for its fantastic modeller and superb render quality.

For this image, I needed to model the background tank, guns and the background ships. The larger models can be quite time-consuming, as I like to paint all of the image maps for each component in Photoshop rather than using procedural textures.

Procedural textures are those that are generated by the 3D software; they have the great advantage of looking good at any resolution, but they tend to have a digital quality to them. Image maps are much more realistic and also give me much more control, especially for a subject like this, as it allows for careful positioning of such details as chipped or damaged paint.

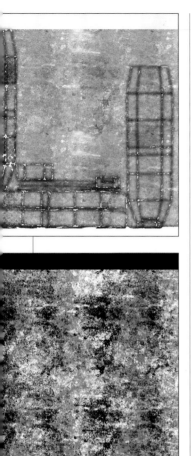

Each component requires at least three texture maps: at the very least a *Colour* map, *Specular* map and *Bump* map. *Colour* determines the colour; *Specular* the shininess of the material; and *Bump* gives an illusion of a raised surface, useful for such things as panel lines or bullet holes.

In addition, it is possible to apply maps to any attribute of a material, such as reflectivity, glossiness, and more. You can find the textures map size getting out of hand if you aren't careful. There are 120.6 megabytes worth of textures on this tank.

4 These are the raw renders from LightWave. I used a *Radiosity* solution and *Area* lights for the tank render. Radiosity is where the software calculates the bounced light from adjacent surfaces, most clearly illustrated by the green reflected light from the grass on the underside of the tank. You also get very realistic soft shadows in any hollows and spaces. *Area* lights most closely approximate a real light source. Usually a light source in a 3D program is an infinitely small single point, a light source that exists nowhere in the natural world. Even the smallest light source in the real world has some size. The net effect of this difference is that, in nature, shadows tend to have some softness, which gets more pronounced the farther away from the object it is cast, and they also get progressively lighter.

A normal 3D single point source light results in a hard, sharp-edged, uniformly toned shadow. That effect was something I used to spend a lot of time correcting in the early days. Even if the software was capable of radiosity, as some were, the hardware was not – not in a usable timeframe anyway. Now, with vastly more powerful machines, available at reasonable cost, all these effects have become feasible to the jobbing illustrator. Still, even with today's technology, the downside to all this realism is the render time. It may look great but still takes an age to render – nine hours in this instance – and I have done renders that take 15 or 20 hours.

Mind you, this is good in comparison with the old, analogue way of doing things – nine hours is much faster than I could have painted it.

5 OK, I now have all the elements I need, so I move into Photoshop to put it all together. I generally work at the finished size at 300dpi unless asked to do otherwise. I can't see the point of working any bigger than necessary. I start with the sky, which in this case was produced by a plug-in for Electric Image, one of the few things I still use EI for. The cloud texture is mapped onto a plane object or polygon, but the basic shapes produced need to be further manipulated and distorted in Photoshop to add a sense of depth. I might just as easily have used one of the hundreds of slides of skies that I have as a starting point.

6 Here I have added some haze and some distant smoke columns, produced by using LightWave's Hypervoxel plug-in. Actually this smoke was rendered for a previous job, but waste-not want-not is what I always say, especially as this is another processor-intensive procedure. I could, of course, choose the easy option and search out a photograph for details like this, but I am loath to use photographic reference directly if I haven't taken it myself. I like the image to be totally my own. This is a personal conceit, since most art directors don't care how the image is produced as long as it's good. For me, it is important that the evironmental and lighting effects remain consistent and believable throughout. There is nothing worse to my eye than an

image derived from photographic elements that have obviously different origins. This doesn't mean that you can't take licence with lighting to produce a particular effect, but it does mean I get to make those decisions based on the composition and aesthetics, rather than being forced into it to accommodate the reference that I have.

7 Now it's time for the tank and grass to go in. This grass is courtesy of the LightWave Sasquatch plug-in. Designed for fur and hair, it does a good job of grass, too. One of the nice things about LightWave is that you get all these plug-ins for free. I've hazed the underside of the tank and, using the *Dodge* tool, over-exposed the middle section to imply light from the gun flashes, which are yet to go in. To get the artwork to match the dynamics of the rough composition some liberties had to be taken with the missile launchers, which, as you can see here, would actually foul the main gun as they turned. However, the figures are going to cover the join; so I don't need to worry overmuch. It's just one of those little problems that arise —

8 Here I've painted in the missile blast. I painted these based on images I trawled from the Internet of real tanks firing. The Internet is a wonderful research tool; I can no longer imagine how I ever managed without it. The black streak of cloud on the right now looks more like smoke from the flames, so I've enhanced that feel.

the rough, drawn freehand for maximum compositional impact, turns out to be impossible when the tank is modelled accurately. Still, I deemed the design the more important of the two aspects, so chose to 'cheat' the tank elements rather than alter it.

11 A few more final touches to the figures. I've darkened them towards the bottom to help concentrate the viewer's eye on the faces, similarly with the foreground grass. I've also added the shadows they should be casting on the ground.

9 The figures finally go in. As you can see if you compare these with the original reference images, a certain amount of work was needed to make the models look like the character description. Described as civilians who have been drawn into war, the male character was dark-skinned and bald, while the female was described as having red hair. I did further work to their features to try and make them more idealized. I generally do most of this work at a larger size on a separate file, to make it easier to paint the details, reducing them later to fit the finished art. This also helps to hide any rough edges that I might have missed. Another advantage of working digitally is that I only need to find models who roughly fit what I have in mind; the *Liquefy* filter in Photoshop has proved to be a most useful tool in this respect.

10 At this point, I turn what I have achieved so far into a background image that I can take into LightWave so as to be able to match position and lighting of the guns. Once it's dropped into the image in Photoshop, I erase any parts of the gun render that should be hidden behind hands or clothing and add any appropriate shadows so as to make them sit convincingly in the hands of the characters. I've added a layer of 'dirt' to the figures to grunge up their clothing a bit. This could be any random texture with a *Gaussian Blur* applied and placed on a layer set to *Multiply*. In this case, it was from a scan of a piece of slate I found in my garden. A small amount of *Motion Blur* added to the male figure's right foot adds to the movement.

12 There are still a few final tweaks: the light on the female character is given a yellow hue, and further adjustments to values and tones are made.

I can really waste a lot of time at this stage as, often at the eleventh hour of a deadline, I will find myself moving elements one millimetre to the right or left, unable to decide which of these microscopic changes improves the image the most.

Finally the aircraft are added, along with the contrails. Once the image is flattened, I make some final overall adjustments to *Color Balance* and *Contrast* before either burning to a CD for postage or, as is becoming ever more likely in these days of broadband, email the job directly to the client.

This is the real revolution of information technology — being able to work from any place in the world and for anyone in the world as long as we both have an Internet connection. I can even have an almost real-time discussion about the way a job is developing, and the client could

just as easily be in the next room or 4,000 miles away. I'm still amazed at this aspect of the new technology when I stop to think about it, and I think it is the single most pronounced change that has taken place, both to the way I work and the opportunities it affords to all of us.

Treasure Hunters

OLIVER HATTON IS A COMPUTER games artist and illustrator based in the southwest of England. Since beginning work in the games industry as a concept artist in 1995, he has worked on numerous successful titles for various companies, including Davilex in Holland, and has worked freelance on many groundbreaking games projects.

Oliver's demonstration, using 3ds max and Photoshop to create an underwater scene, will show you how easy it can be to create quite simple, yet very effective, results with only a limited knowledge of 2D and 3D packages.

'Because the many 3D modelling packages on the market can often use different terminology or techniques to arrive at the same result, I believe it is more efficient (in terms of space in this book) to assume that you are familiar with some of the basic modelling techniques.

"I apologize if some sections seem incomprehensible, but it may help to consult your user manual to see if it demonstrates something similar. Otherwise you can experiment. This is no series of expert step-by-step modelling prompts for you to follow. These are guidelines to one possible approach. You won't need the latest version of that 3D modelling or drawing package, either.

"One of the best things about working on computers, especially in 3D, is the ability to adapt work as it progresses. At any time, you can modify a part or delete it, or just keep a bit you like and work from that. This is great, because you can permanently retain the ability to change a major aspect of the scene or, say, radically change your viewpoint with ease.

'Unless the brief says "…and with an incredibly detailed background", you can begin very quickly to create great atmospheric scenes with the simplest of textures, and without trying, to emulate vast environmental effects by fiddling for hours or days (depending on the power of your computer), tweaking atmospheric settings in a complex file.

'There is no single correct route in this process, but there are easier or quicker ways to reach the same point. If you think ahead about how you are going to approach the matter, then many obstacles may not even arise.'

SOFTWARE **3DS MAX, PHOTOSHOP** ARTIST **OLIVER HATTON** WEBSITE **WWW.OLDROID.COM** EMAIL **HATTON@CAIROMAIL.COM**

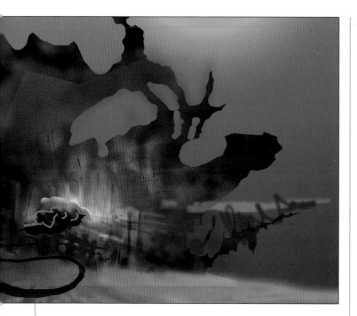

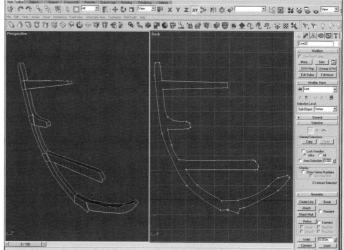

1 I often try to begin the concept work with a series of extremely rapid, rough doodles that really make no sense to anyone. I can mess around for hours, adding parts of scribble to random lines, combining other doodles on the page, or rubbing pieces away, sheet after sheet, until I begin to develop a semblance of something I like the look of, perhaps an atmospheric landscape or a spaceship, or a building or piece of anatomy. It's quite easy to come up with a set of completely irrelevant images after several hours doodling. You must continue to push the pencil or cursor around, looking for what you're after.

Eventually, I'll get a rough idea of a composition together, and, possibly apply some colours in a 2D package or just work the

idea up, to give the rough concept some volume.

At this point, I'll begin thinking of how I'll construct the image in 3D. As this was an underwater scene, I could make the setting fairly vague. Like in misty jungles, cloudy cities or sand-blown deserts, detail other than vague form can often be quickly lost. Because of this, the models didn't need to be either especially complex, or especially neatly constructed. They just needed to fade into the surrounding environment and look convincing. Building a scene in which you are going to animate is a completely different matter — then the models must be neat, because every flaw in the model will have a greater chance of being inspected as the viewer's point of view changes.

2 I began by creating the ancient, wrecked ship hull that would be in the foreground.

Very rapidly I created a cross-section contour of the hull's

wooden beams with an *Editable Spline*, and then lofted it a little to give it some depth. This was to be the beginning of the skeleton of the ship's hull.

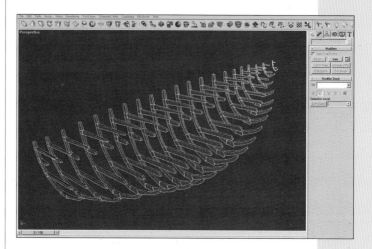

3 I copied it many times at support beam distances until I had a tubular ribcage of wooden beams. I attached all of the objects together and converted the object into an *Editable Mesh*. From here, at sub-object level, I scaled down each

end on various axes, using *Soft Selection* (in 3ds max), and moved them around a little, to try to create a smooth hull shape. The most important point is that your model is convincing enough from any angle that you might see it from.

3

4 Then, with the aid of *3D Vertex Snap*, I created a *Spline Cage* (a shape made of splines in 3D space, in 3ds max) to make the outer skin of the ship. This *Spline Cage* had its points snapped to vertices on the ship mesh, which roughly matched up with an imaginary set of contour lines that could best describe the basic shape of the skin. I knew this skin would hardly be visible, just something to catch shadows and add to the scene, and so again the level of detail here wasn't so important.

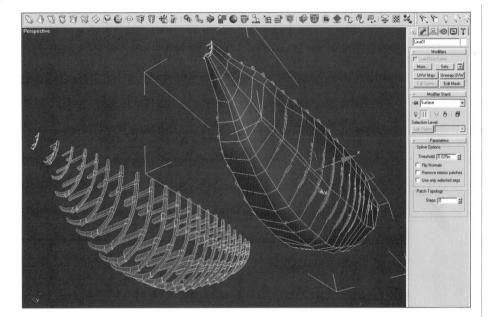

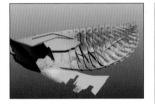

5 After applying a *Surface Tools Modifier*, I converted it into an *Editable Mesh*, and, in *Sub Object Mode* copied all of the faces as an *Element*, flipped the new faces to *Normals* and *Extruded* them, to give the surface some depth. I then converted it into an *Editable Mesh* and deleted certain faces to add a little detail as the ragged outer shell of the ship. After placing and attaching a few edited simple objects, I converted it all into a single object. Then I applied a basic standard material to the object (which I later gave a small amount of noise), and that was it. I had a simple wrecked ship.

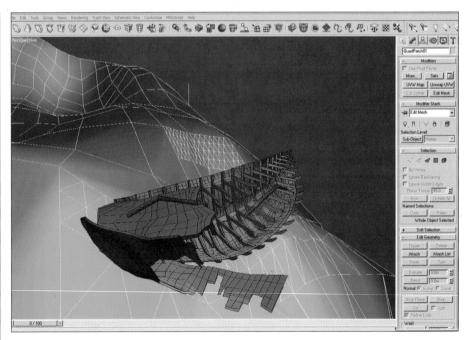

6 The seabed was originally a *Quad Patch*, and I pushed and pulled some of the vertices, predominantly on a vertical axis, to suit the shape that the sea floor took in my composition sketch. Finally, I began tessellating specific areas of faces within the plane, subdividing and smoothing areas that were relevant to important points on the sea bed and tweaking those, basically making it look less angular. I gave it a similar texture that I had applied to the ship.

7 I put a camera in the scene with a few lights and changed some environmental settings, like the ambient colours and levels, to try to generate some simple underwater atmosphere. The background is a gradient used as a *Background* map.

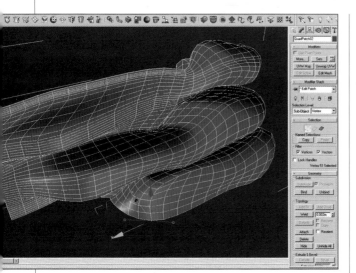

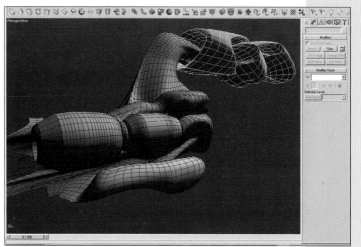

8 Now I needed to build the spaceship. Again, being conscious of the angle from which I would see the craft, I was aware that it wouldn't be necessary to create the entire thing. From the outset, I created only half a model, as I created a left-right mirrored instance of my object. This helps me to see the model take shape instantly in symmetry, which is useful in making design choices and is a great time-saver. I began with a basic *Quad Patch*, moving groups of vertices around and manipulating *Bezier Handles* to try to create the folds and volume of the craft. I added *Quad Patches* to certain edges of the patch to extend areas of the model, until again I eventually had a shape that was similar to the shape in my concept sketch.

9 The head was simply stuck on from a rotated, copied part of the model. Patches can be great fun to work with and are fantastic at helping create organic forms. Just practising adjusting *Bezier Handles* and adding *Quad* or *Tri Patches* to a patch edge can help enormously, however, and you can learn to build complex shapes. The decaying circular tanks or thrusters on the side of the craft were rapidly made by deleting faces from an editable set of concentric cylinders that had been lathed out of a spline.

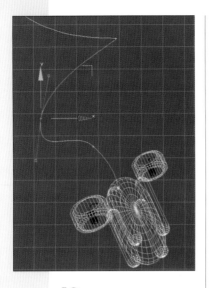

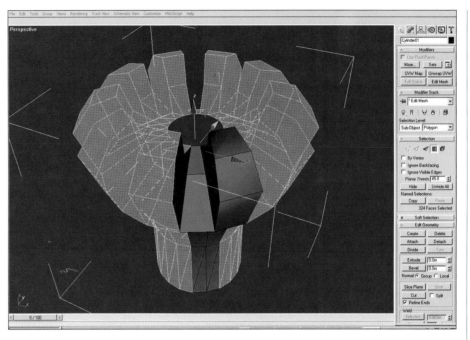

10 The R.O.V. (remote operated vehicle) above the wrecked ship is a collection of standard and extended primitive objects (a squashed sphere, four capsules and some cylinders) with a plain texture applied to them. They have a *Renderable Spline* remote control cord trailing away from them towards the camera.

11 The ocean-bed alien city was begun by selecting two segments of a cylinder and making a crenellated shape. I deleted the other faces and then rotated the looping shape around its now free-floating axis, to make a crenellated tower like a vast mechanical coral polyp.

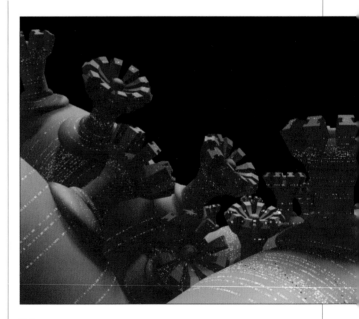

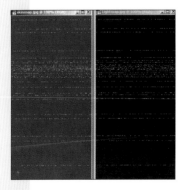

12 This sat on two intersecting squashed spheres. I then applied a texture (made in Photoshop) of little dotted lights on a plain blue background, and made a *Self-Illumination* map by making a copy of the texture, *De-saturating* it, then amplifying the *Contrast*.

13 I made many copies of this and attached them to a set of similarly textured cylinders that had a *Bend Modifier* on them.

3

15 Although the scene is relatively empty, I tried to fill the camera's view with interesting and somehow balanced (pleasingly, or uncomfortably, for example) shapes, texture and colour. I find I change the camera position fairly frequently when building scenes. But also moving objects around in the scene can be very effective when your goal is a 2D image.

Another good way to develop composition is to create a larger scene, then crop the image down to a desired final image later when you have a better understanding of the contents. One of the great bonuses of using 3D software to make 2D work is the opportunity to take advantage of 2D art packages. Because of the extreme F.O.V. in the scene, I built and rendered the background alien city in a separate file, trying to keep the lighting and colour values the same, and merged the images in Photoshop. Again, this may seem pretty rough, but if you're after a 2D result it saves lots of time. Very quickly, I managed to generate additional atmosphere by adding touches of detail, and using filter effects and HSB changes, often in selected areas. I always work on copies of layers, and within selection areas copied to a new layer, because you can experiment more freely. The rotten sails were drawn on. It's true that I could have created a mesh sail and applied a texture with an alpha map to it, but I was unsure at the time how I wanted that area to look, and this was a very quick solution. Maybe if I made it again I would do it all differently. The main points to emphasize are belief in your goal, practice, experimentation and perseverance (and realizing when to stop). Good luck.

14 The majority of the hard work in this scene is done by the camera and light placing, with *Lighting Colour*, and with the environment settings, such as the *Ambient Colour* and the *Global Lighting Hue* and *Brightness*. By manipulating these, it's possible to obtain incredible variations in the scene's appearance. When I was adjusting them, I tried to remain aware of general environmental hues, keeping my palette suited to an underwater theme. The camera developed a wider and wider F.O.V. (field of view) as the image took shape.

I liked the underwater fish-eye feeling, and thought that it really emphasized the ripped-open belly of the ancient ship, glowing under the R.O.V.'s lights. This then lead into the image of another antiquated wreck from a distant planet. The composition is an incredibly important aspect of the final result.

Planet Life

IN THE SECOND OF OLIVER HATTON'S step-by-step tutorials, he creates a striking scene using 3ds max and Photoshop. Alien worlds have always proved an inspirational and challenging subject for artists to visualize, and this dynamic view of a gleaming city, juxtaposed within a mysterious fungoid landscape, is suitably atmospheric. As Oliver reveals, it's a surprisingly simple scene created using only a very basic set of objects, along with just four simple textures, all made to look more complex with clever use of composition and lighting. Various short-cuts show how to quickly achieve effective results that are ideally suited to a static scene of this sort, especially when facing a tight deadline or if you have only a fairly basic knowledge of 3D software.

1 With a very limited amount of time available, I needed to create an atmospheric alien landscape. With this in mind, I began jotting down a few extremely rough digital sketches in Photoshop to work out a composition, and to gather some understanding (in terms of colour and shape) of what I was trying to aim at, and very shortly afterwards began working on a 2D sky image for the background of the 3D scene in the same program.

SOFTWARE 3DS MAX, PHOTOSHOP ARTIST OLIVER HATTON
WEBSITE WWW.OLDROID.COM EMAIL HATTON@CAIROMAIL.COM

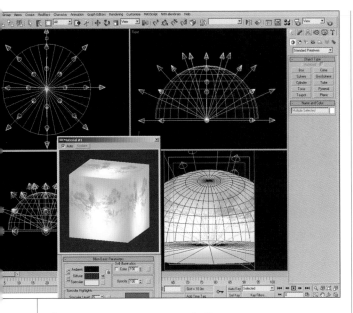

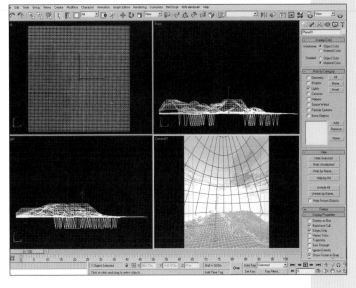

2 The sky texture was very rapidly created, as I knew most of the background would be obscured by the rest of the objects in the scene. I find that a good way of making clouds in 2D for a sky texture is to block-in a few colours in rough cloud-type shapes, and then push and pull these shapes around with various sizes and strengths of the *Smudge* tool brush. To pick out extra details on the textures, I used the *Lighting Effects* filter in Photoshop with *Directional* or *Omni* lighting, and used a *Texture Channel* colour in the *Lighting Effects* options to give the texture some 'bump-type' effect.

3 Only three other textures were used in the scene: one for the mushrooms, one for the rock surface and another for the moon. The rest of the objects basically have a standard material assigned to them with an appropriate colour, and sometimes to get the right effect, a little self illumination on the material can help. Most of the textures on objects in this scene are self-illuminated to some degree or other. I don't think that it's always good to do this, but sometimes it can be pretty helpful in a simple scene. The sky dome to which the sky texture is applied is 100% self illuminated. The sky dome is special in another way, too, in that in its *Properties* panel I turned the *Receive* and *Cast Shadows* buttons to off, and the *Specular Highlights* are set to zero.

4 Imagine if you made a landscape of 'hillside-shaped' extruded splines that were stacked behind each other to represent hills disappearing off into the horizon, then used the *Eyedropper* tool on a real photograph to capture the RGB values of real-life colours of a landscape on a hazy day, and applied the correct colour to each 'hillside' plane. Although the whole scene would consist of only a handful of polys, it could seem quite realistic, just because the colours were convincing. It's definitely worth giving it a go.

The scene used in this demonstration is actually a very basic set of objects that are built to look more complicated by composing the objects in the scene at the time of placing them, using the camera viewport to position them. This is a really quick and neat way of building up your composition when you're not creating a scene that needs to be animated.

It's worth mentioning at this point that it's good to try to stick to one single scale system when working in 3D. This can go a long way towards preventing the kinds of crazy scaling problems that can otherwise occur. If you do bend the rules in a scene, at least you are aware of where and why this is then happening.

I began the scene by building the distant, hilly landscape with a plane several kilometres across that had a few hundred width and length segments (you can always optimize this landscape later), which I then gave an *Edit Mesh* modifier.

I then began to pull selected areas of vertices at sub-object level on the Z-axis (vertically) only, with *Affect Region* on and set to various strengths on the *Falloff* spinner, to manipulate different scales of the landscape at any one time. For example, the base of the hill had a large falloff value compared to the peaks.

3

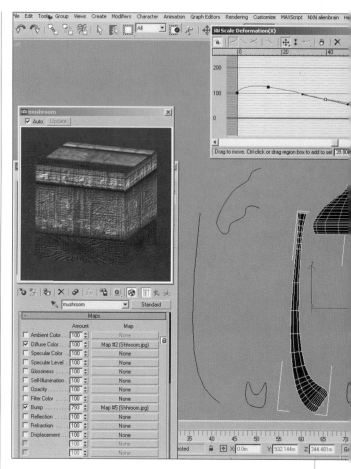

5 When I'd done this, I applied a default material and began constructing a basic 'city' style structure out of many variously sized, standard, primitive boxes, which were placed on some cylinders. I attached all of these objects together and applied the same standard material that I'd given to the hills.

The distant structure is basically a much simpler version of the closer one. After creating the towers, I then positioned them so that they stood on the hills.

The foreground land is a separate plane that received the same treatment but on a smaller scale, with one of the four textures that I'd made up in Photoshop earlier applied to it. In the *Maps* section in the *Material Editor* in 3ds max, I copied the *Diffuse* map onto the *Bump* map slot and turned up the *Bump* values to give them a rougher texture. I did this with all the textures I made in this scene.

To give the scene a softer feeling, I created a half-sphere of about 25 inward-facing instanced spotlights with a wide hotspot and an even wider *Falloff* setting, set to cast shadows, and with the intensity setting very low (about 0.02 on the *Multiplier*).

6 The other lights in the scene consist of the 'sun' – a target spot facing the camera, which is obscured by the closest of the two building structures – and several omni lights that all illuminate the scene from beneath. These omni lights are set at a variety of intensities and colours and they are also set to include or exclude certain objects, so that I can then control the lighting on various objects individually. For instance, the foreground objects are lit with a very intense turquoise light that is set up so that it does not affect the distant objects.

7 The mushrooms were created by lathing a spline for the cap and then lofting a closed spline along another curved, open spline for the stem. The loft was tweaked in the *Deformations* section in the *Modifier* panel so that it tapered as it went upwards by altering the *Scale* 'line'. I tried to improve its shape by adding *Corner Points* along the line and moving them around with the points' properties set to be *Bezier-Smooth* until I had a shape that was a little bit more organic.

The mushroom texture I made was applied in sections (top and bottom of the cap, and then the stem) and the *Bump Mapping Spinner* in the *Material Editor* was cranked up. The cap was attached to the stem and then copied around the scene, using the camera viewport to place them. The camera viewport has a fairly wide field of view. The little, rounded objects on the floor surrounding the mushrooms, which look like soft, inflatable cacti, were made by attaching half-spheres around a lathed spline that was shaped a bit like a question mark. Smaller copies of this object were attached to the cap of the parent version, as if they were newer, growing

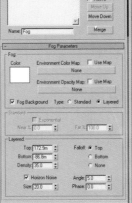

branches. These 'cactoids' were given a *Multi/Sub-Object* material; one for the flesh, and one for the half-sphere nodes, which were given a different *Sub-Object Face ID*. The fleshy part of the material was given a small amount of self-illumination (14%). This was then copied and placed around the scene, using the camera viewport to guide my choice in positioning them.

8 Swirling around the toes of the giant city structures are two sets of layered fog, one set to fade to nothing at 170 metres high and the other set to fade off 70 metres lower. If you layer the fog like this, it helps to increase the subtlety of the effect, in my opinion. Finally, I added the glowing lights on the tower.

9 This was a fairly dense cage of omni-light instances with *Lens Effects > Glow* applied to them. Basically, that was it. When I was building this scene, I rendered fairly frequent test images at a lower resolution (800x600) to see how my scene was building up. The image finally paid a brief visit to Photoshop, where I brushed off a couple of the most annoying blemishes.

When I read back through this workthrough, it seems somewhat crude to work in this way, but sometimes it can really pay off. This is particularly true if your schedule is very tight and especially so if your final image is static rather than an animation.

Anti-matter Spacecraft

NICHOLAS HALLIDAY IS A DESIGNER, illustrator, author and actor. His first book, *21ˢᵗ Century Space Missions,* became an international bestseller. His passions are for the past and the future, which are kept alive by both his work and his growing family.

Maxon's Cinema 4D is a high-end modelling, rendering and animation program. This illustration was produced in Release 8 on a duel processor 1GHz G4 Macintosh. In addition to the usual polygon and terrain objects, deformers, environments and lighting, C4D's most powerful modelling tools are NURBS. These are generators, not objects, which means they use other objects to generate their surfaces. Some 90% of the objects in this illustration use NURBS and it is only by understanding these that you will get the best from C4D modelling. In learning how to model these parts, the reader is required to possess a basic knowledge of 3D design and of C4D.

Here Nick explains how he constructed the main engine of an antimatter craft included in his latest book, *21ˢᵗ Century Space: The Definitive Guide to Future Space Missions.*

'The illustration was researched by looking at the current interpretations of anti-matter engines produced by independent and agency illustrators (such as those working at NASA). It was from these, and further reading about how anti-matter propulsion would actually work, that I designed my own craft. The process was an organic one and the illustration began with an idea in mind rather than a sketch. This helped the illustration remain fluid and allowed me to adjust the ideas when unusual or interesting events were revealed during modelling.

'The vast majority of the objects were first drawn in a vector (or line) based program. Personally, I favour Adobe Illustrator. The files can then easily be imported into C4D and used within NURBS. In order to do this, there needs to be a certain amount of "thinking ahead" – knowing how you are going to produce each object will dictate how your base line drawings are finished.'

SOFTWARE **CINEMA 4D** ARTIST **NICHOLAS HALLIDAY** WEBSITE **WWW.HALLIDAYBOOKS.COM** EMAIL **INFO@HALLIDAYBOOKS.COM**

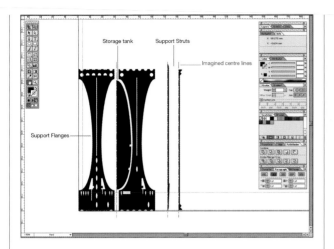

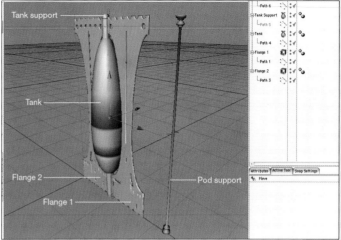

1 Create a new project folder and call it 'Antimatter Engine'. The following parts are drawn together but will be used in different ways by C4D. The storage tanks and support struts will be cylindrical (or lathe) objects and the support flanges will be flat (or extruded) objects. Therefore, you need to draw flat faces for the support flanges and half profiles for the storage tanks and support flanges, with the imagined centre line on the left of the object. Position the vector-drawn elements in the bottom left of the page (C4D imports this point to where its X, Y and Z axes meet). Title this file 'Engine Parts 1' and save it in your project folder as an EPS file.

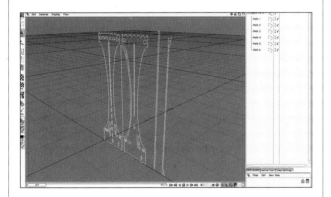

2 Open C4D. In the main window go to *File > Open*, then locate the project folder and open 'Engine Parts 1'. You will see your object appear in the viewport, and a folder called 'Engine Parts 1', containing your paths, will appear in the object manager. Save this file as 'Antimatter Engine.c4d' in your project folder.

3 Drag each item from the folder so they sit independently in the *Object Manager*, then delete the original folder. Locate each piece and name them accordingly: 'Flange 1', 'Flange 2', 'Tank', 'Tank support' and 'Pod support'. Add an *Extrude* NURBS object to the scene and place the 'Flange 1' path within it. The path will immediately extrude. Select the NURBS, select *Object* in the *Attribute Manager,* then type '1' into the *Movement* box. Select *Caps* in the *Attribute Manager*, select *Fillet Cap* on both *Start* and *End* and type '1' into both *Steps* and *Radius* boxes. Select *Linear* as the *Fillet* type. Repeat these steps for the 'Flange 2' path. Add a *Lathe* NURBS to the scene and place the 'Tank' path within it.

The path will immediately rotate about the central Y-axis. View the scene from the top, (*View > View 2*). With the path (not the NURBS) selected, choose the *Move Active Element* tool and drag the red X-axis arrow to the left until the inside edges of the tank meet at their centre. View the scene from the front (*View > View4*) and then, with the 'Tank' *Lathe* NURBS selected, drag the red X-axis arrow to the right until the tank sits back within the support flanges. Repeat this process with two further *Lathe* NURBS for the 'Tank Support' and the 'Pod Support'. 'Tank Support' runs through the centre of the tank and holds the Storage tanks to the Flanges. 'Pod Support' holds the flanges to the central engine pod.

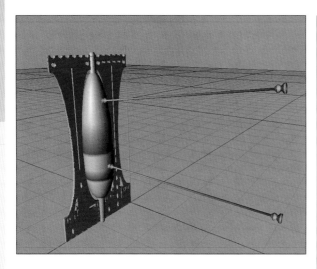

4 Select the 'Pod Support' NURBS and rotate it 90° about the X-axis, then position one end of the support against the tank – about two-thirds of the way down. Duplicate the 'Pod Support' and position this about two-thirds of the way up the tank, then rotate it a further 8° about the X-axis (to 98°). Group these two 'Pod Supports' with 'Tank 1' and 'Tank Support' and collect them to a new *Null* object and name it 'Tank/Supports 1'.

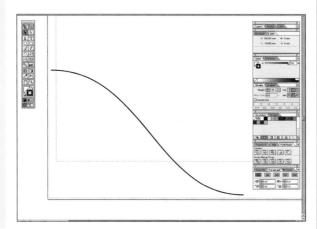

5 In your vector-based program, draw a simple curved line as shown in the above image, and then save it out as 'Pipeline.eps' in your project folder.

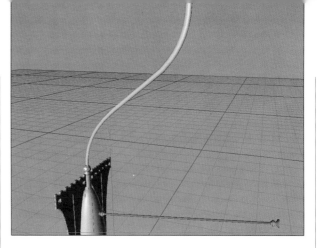

6 Import 'Pipeline.eps' into C4D. Add a *Sweep* NURBS to your scene, call it 'Pipe' and drop the 'Pipeline' path into it. Add a circle spline from the *Spline* menu and drop this into the *Sweep* NURBS. The NURBS will sweep the circle alone the 'Pipeline' path to create a tube. You will need to resize the circle spline to make the pipe appear as it does here. In the *Attribute Manager*, select *Object* and type 200% in the *Scaling* box and 100% in the *Growth* box. This will taper the tube. To create the junction joint for the pipe, add a *Platonic* object to the scene. Name it 'Joint'. Select the *Object* tab in the *Attribute Manager* and choose *Bucky* as *Type*. Reduce the size of the 'Joint' object to fit on the end of the pipe. Group and collect 'Joint' and 'Pipe' and name this new *Null* object 'Joint/Pipe'. View the scene from above (and the side) and position the 'Joint/Pipe' on the top point of 'Tank Support'.

7 Surface textures for these parts will be simple, as the light source within the engine will create all the drama. Select *File > New material* from the *Materials Manager* and call it 'Tank'. Enable *Colour* and choose a mid-blue at 100% *Brightness*. Enable *Reflection* and select 100% for R, G, and B, and 50% on the *Brightness* slider. Enable *Specular* and choose *Metal* mode, then adjust *Width* and *Height* to 80%. Copy this texture and call it 'Supports'. In *Colour*, select 100% for R, G, and B and drag the *Brightness* slider to 0%, leaving the remaining options as they are. Copy this texture and call it 'Flanges'.

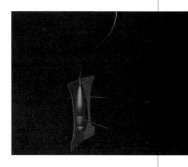

In *Colour*, drag the *Brightness* slider to 50%; in *Reflection*, drag the *Brightness* slider to 20%; and then in *Specular*, choose *Plastic* mode and drag the *Height* slider to 40%. Apply the textures: material *Tank* to 'Tank'; *Supports* to 'Tank Supports', 'Pod Supports', 'Pipe' and 'Joint'; and finally material *Flanges* to 'Flanges'.

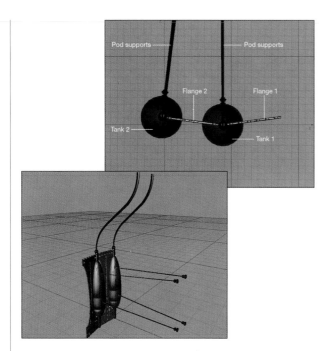

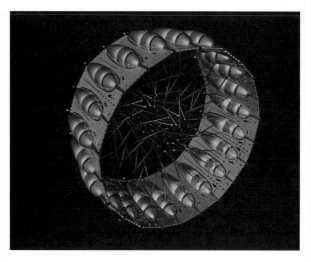

8 Drop the 'Pipe' group into 'Tank/Support 1' group and duplicate 'Tank Support 1'. Rename it 'Tank/Support 2' and drag this to its new position within the space at the end of 'Flange 2', as shown. Select 'Flange 1' and rotate it +7.5° on the X-axis (you can do this under *Rotation* in the *Coordinates Manager* by typing 7.5° in the *H* box). Then drag 'Flange 2' into the 'Tank/Support 2' group and rotate the whole group –7.5° (again, you can do this under *Rotation* in the *Coordinates Manager* by typing –7.5° into the *H* box). You will need to reposition the two groups slightly so that they meet the centre of the tanks properly. Select and group all objects and name the new *Null* object 'Engine parts 1'.

9 Add an *Array* object to your scene, name it 'Engine array' and then drop 'Engine parts 1' into it. The group will immediately duplicate around the central Y-axis using the *Array* object

default options. In the *Attribute Manager*, under the *Objects* tab, type '200' into the *Radius* box (you will need to adjust this for your own drawing). Type '10' into the *Copies* box.

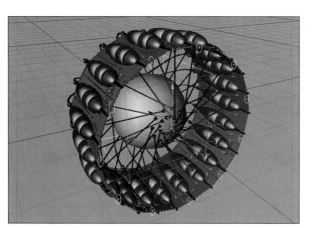

10 Add a *HyperNURBS* object and a *Cube* object to your scene. Name the *HyperNURBS* 'Central hub' and drop the *Cube* object into it. The *Cube* object will immediately turn into a rough sphere. Select the *NURBS* and under the *Object* tab in the *Attributes Manager* type '4' in both *Subdivision Editor* and *Subdivision Render* boxes (this will help to smooth the object). Select the *Cube* object (not the NURBS) and select *Structure > Make Editable*. The cube symbol in the Object manager will then turn into a small blue triangle. In the toolbar select the *Polygon* tool and, with the cube still selected, select the front face.

3

11 Drag the red X-Axis arrow over to the right to form an oval about three times the original length of the sphere. Then select *Structure > **Extrude Inner*** and drag your mouse over to the left a little way to create a small inner polygon. Repeat this process to make a third polygon at about the same distance.

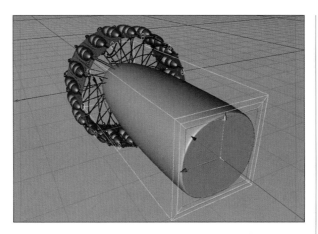

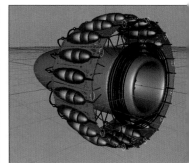

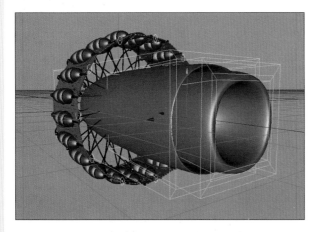

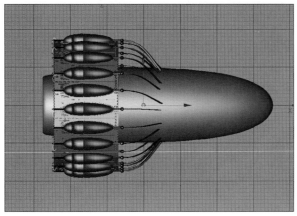

12 Drag the red X-axis arrow to the left about half way back inside the object. A tunnel will appear as you do this. Select *Structure > **Extrude Inner*** and drag your mouse to the left a little. Then drag the red X-axis arrow back out to the right. You will see the inner bulb come back up the tube. Select *Structure > **Extrude Inner*** again and drag your mouse to the left a little, release, drag to the left a little, release and finally drag to the left a little (three separate repeated operations). Lastly, drag the red X-axis arrow to the left and you will see the end of the bulb travel back down the tube, creating a second inner tube. View the scene from the side (*View > **View 2***), select 'Central Hub' and drag it back into the engine array until about half of the inner tube sits just outside the array. Apply the material 'Flange' to the central hub.

13 To create the heat sinks, add a *Tube* object to your scene and name it 'Heat Sink'. Adjust the object to be fine and flat and fit it closely to (but not touching) the end of the inner tube on your central hub. Duplicate the heat sink five times and space them close to each other to form a neat set of rings. Group and collect the rings and call the new *Null* object 'Heat Sink'. Duplicate this and enlarge it so that it sits just outside the first set, then repeat this process to form a third set of rings. Group and collect all three sets and name them 'Heat Sinks'. Finally, apply the material 'Supports' to the heat sinks.

3

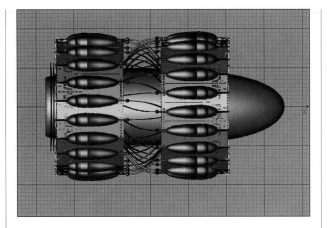

14 Duplicate the 'Engine Array' group, rotate it 180° and slide it down the central hub to sit just behind its sister array.

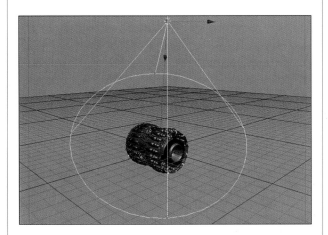

15 Add a light source with a target to your scene (this will help illuminate the outer engine parts when you apply the inner engine light). Pull the light target to the centre of your model and the light source some way off (so that it throws an even light over the whole model).

16 Add a light source to your scene, name it 'Centre' and centre it within the end of the inner tube of the central hub. In the *Attributes Manager* under the *General* tab, select a light blue colour and apply 70% *Brightness*. *Type*: *Omni*, *Shadow*: *Hard*, *Visible Light*: *Visible*, *Noise*: *None*. Check the boxes for *Show Illumination*, *Show Visible Light* and *Show Clipping*. Under the *Visibility* tab, type *Brightness*: 200% and *Dust*: 100%. Under the *Shadow* tab, select 60% *Density*. The *Visible Light Indicator* should reach just inside the tanks. Under the *Visible* tab, type 200% in the *Brightness* box and uncheck the *Adapt Brightness* box. Under the *Noise* tab, type: *Wavy*, turbulence, *Octaves*; 4, *Velocity*, 25%, *Brightness*; -30%, and *Contrast*, 150%.

Duplicate this light and call it 'Corona'. Extend the *Visible Light Indicator* to reach just outside the tanks. In the *Attributes Manager*, change: *Brightness*, 100%, *Shadow*, *None*; *Noise*, *Visibility*. Under the *Visibility* tab, change

Brightness: 250% and check the *Adapt Brightness* box. Under the *Noise* tab, change: *Brightness*, –30%; and *Contrast*, 150%.

Duplicate this light and call it 'Plasma'. Extend the *Visible Light Indicator* to a little way beyond the perimeters of the model. In the *Attributes Manager* under the *Visibility* tab, change the *Brightness* to 200%. Under the *Noise* tab, set: *Brightness* to –300%; and *Contrast*: to 500%.

Finally, group and collect the three light sources and name the *Null* object 'Engine Light'. Now render the model.

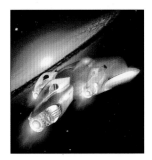

A New World of Gods and Monsters

Horror artwork usually has a direct and focused intention: to stir in the viewer a sense of unease and something approaching the thrill of terror. Often these are immediate and confrontational nightmare images, playing upon our phobias and designed to provoke a definite reaction. They allow us to safely indulge ourselves in the very basic human instinct of fear. These can be pictures that provide a passport to the dark side of our nature and our age-old inheritance of being afraid of what might lurk in the shadows.

4

Left: An illustration from 1909 by the great American illustrator, Howard Pyle, for *The Salem Wolf*, a story he also wrote.

Right: Matthias Grünewald (c.1460-1528) created a nightmare scene of horror in *The Temptations of St Anthony*. This altarpiece was obviously intended to frighten worshippers with its interpretation of damnation.

AS AN ARTIST I'VE ALWAYS LOVED THE MACABRE. As soon as I could wield a crayon, no wallpaper was safe from my drawings of malignant monsters. It might be my first memory of television that was the cause, which just happened to be an episode of *Doctor Who*. This set me off on a splendidly terror-filled journey with the series throughout my formative years, memories of which remain resonant and hugely inspirational.

There's always been such a rich vein of macabre and shocking artwork to confront and captivate us. A strong tradition, taking us from the Gothic chapbooks of the early 19th century, through the 'penny dreadfuls' and Victorian sensational fiction, to the era of the pulp magazines, the controversial EC (Entertaining Comics) horror comics of the '50s, and beyond.

One of my favourite early artists to become synonymous with horror was Harry Clarke, who is famed for his illustrated 1919 edition of Edgar Allan Poe's *Tales of Mystery and Imagination*. There are strong similarities in style with the drawings of his contemporary, Aubrey Beardsley, but at their best Clarke's illustrations contain strange, elongated forms composed of dense and claustrophobic patterns.

An important sub-genre of horror art that has a long and rich history, is devoted to H. P. Lovecraft's *Cthulhu Mythos* stories. A great many brilliant artists have illustrated these cosmic horror tales with their dread depictions of blasphemous eldritch things that no mortal eyes were ever meant to see.

Three great artists readily come to mind, each of whom contributed to pulp-era magazines such as the legendary *Weird Tales*. Virgil Finlay's beautifully rendered pen and ink illustrations have been an endless inspiration. The stylized work of Hannes Bok has been another favourite; one of his finest illustrations was drawn for Lovecraft's story *Pickman's Model*. Also for the pulps, and later for the weird fiction publisher Arkham House, the work of Lee Brown Coye has been influential, the distorted shapes in his art perfectly conveying the mood of macabre fantasy.

Coming much more up-to-date, the Lovecraftian artwork of Dave Carson has continued the tradition of the pulp era illustrators, and he is an artist who has made the transition to capturing his tentacled nightmare creatures digitally, as we'll see in this section.

Jack Davis is renowned for his gruesome artwork on *Tales from the Crypt* and *The Vault of Horror*, two of the famed EC horror comics of the 1950s. Davis and other EC artists have proved to be extremely influential in this genre, particularly on the flesh-dripping work of Berni Wrightson, a true master of the macabre. His wonderfully atmospheric artwork for a 1983 edition of Mary Shelley's *Frankenstein* perfectly evoked the entire sweep and decayed grandeur of the Gothic romance. Wrightson's film work has included the EC tribute *Creepshow*, for which his style was ideally suited.

There are far too many great artists to mention, even just in passing, in a potted personal background to the horror genre like this. But there are one or two others whose work should at least be touched upon, not least of these is H. R. Giger.

The work of this nightmare surrealist has changed the face of horror and science fiction today , particularly through his production design on *Alien*. His beautifully airbrushed and deeply erotic biomechanical monstrosities offer a potent mixture of attraction and repulsion.

Les Edwards has been another favourite in recent years. His paintings can often be very full-blooded and visceral, with graphic depictions of flesh-eating monsters, but are also capable of conveying great supernatural menace in more subtle images inspired by classic ghost stories.

Perhaps the first artist working in fantasy to use photographic morphing has been J. K. Potter, heralding the transition to digital techniques. His images assault the eye with their realism, depicting mutations of the human body and unlikely objects in uneasy alliances with flesh.

There are countless other inspiring and individual artists who have enriched and developed the horror genre with their imagery throughout its history. With the development of digital techniques, artists now have a whole new set of tools with which to breathe life into things from their, and our, worst nightmares.

Cthulhu, one of H. P. Lovecraft's pantheon of dark gods, by renowned Cthulhu Mythos horror artist Dave Carson.

A 1936 cover for *Astounding Stories* by Howard V. Brown, illustrating H. P. Lovecraft's *The Shadow Out of Time*.

The Tank

THIS IMAGE WAS ONE OF MANY that I produced as part of the original concept material for the forthcoming Gothic horror computer game *Frankenstein's Legions*, and it was also used as part of the original design document and initial pitch for the game.

The original idea stemmed from a conversation I had with the designer of the game, Dave Morris. We were thinking of how to depict an atmospheric and horror-filled scene inside a laboratory, and thought it would be fun to see a couple of 'scientists' staring, in fascination or perhaps revulsion, straight at the viewer. We decided that with a shift of focus, the viewer would see the reflection of what the distressed scientists were looking at, and realize that the scene was observed from the point of view of something nasty floating behind the glass of one of the tanks in the scientists' laboratory. An unpleasant sense of what their monstrous creation would see as it came alive – and the reaction of the two hapless characters as something unimaginable is going wrong with their experiment.

1 As always, I began with a rough concept sketch outlining the very vaguest idea of a composition. All I had in mind was that I wanted the figures fairly close-up, somehow peering towards the viewer, and slightly distorted by the liquid and the glass of the tank through which they are viewed. I wasn't at all sure how to tackle the scene, having some concerns about how it might easily become cluttered and confusing, what with needing to see the characters clearly, as well as a suggestion of the laboratory beyond and its assorted scientific apparatus – all viewed through the distortion of the glass, while somehow allowing the reflection to be visible in front of everything else.

SOFTWARE **PHOTOSHOP** ARTIST **MARTIN MCKENNA** WEBSITE **WWW.MARTINMCKENNA.NET** EMAIL **MARTIN@MARTINMCKENNA.NET**

2 I carried on regardless and set up a quick photo-shoot, posing models to roughly conform to both my original concept sketch and the overall image that I had in mind.

From these, I then produced some very quick pencil sketches and scanned them in at 300dpi, saving them as PSDs as a background layer that I could then work on top of.

3 In Photoshop, I opened a new layer on each of the character sketches, and started to work on each one as a line drawing. Working extremely rapidly, I simply used the *Airbrush* tool with two or three small sizes of brush, with black as the foreground colour at 100% pressure. I also alternated with white to tidy some of the lines as I went, add some

highlights, and to draw over the black lines in places to create softer hatching for blends. All this produced the appearance of a fairly traditional ink drawing. My thinking at this stage was that I wanted the picture to have a slightly linear appearance, and to reproduce something of the feel of the old traditional 'line and wash' colour illustrations that I used to do.

4 I now brought the two drawings together, dragging them onto a single canvas and using the *Transform* tool to re-size them so that they were in scale with each other. I then used the *Move* tool to place them where I thought that they might work best. I positioned the figure on the right behind the left-hand figure, and used the *Eraser* tool to remove the part of his elbow that was overlapping. I then merged the two layers into one master. I'd prepared a basic scanned watercolour texture background at this stage, as although I was

still very much 'feeling my way' with the picture, I didn't want to start work on a sterile white canvas. The blobby shapes might also make it into the final scene, perhaps as part of the liquid in the tank. I made it green using *Image > Adjust > Hue/Saturation*, because I knew that I wanted the scene to be lit by a predominantly green light – as, of course, all proper ungodly things in jars just should be. Because I'd drawn the line work on its own layer, it allowed the colour to show through. I now had a base on which to work on the figures.

5 Next, I started to paint the highlights onto the figures, using a new layer above the line work. I sketched in the highlights using a small hard-edged airbrush with a very light green tone. This is one of my favourite drawing techniques and it is great to use it in Photoshop. I wanted the figures to be lit from below, as though from the tank or by some other piece of glowing scientific apparatus nearby. And in the true tradition of melodramatic Gothic horror film lighting, I wanted to achieve a similar flavour to the under-lighting used in *Bride of*

Frankenstein for almost every appearance of Ernest Thesiger's fantastically portrayed Dr. Praetorious. I also darkened the background a little to heighten this eerie glowing effect.

6 I now started to apply some colour to the figures on another new layer. I started to block-in my basic colour choices using a hard-edged brush, and then using the *Smudge* tool to blend them. A lot of the detailing and modelling of the shapes was taken care of by the dark and light line work on the upper layers, meaning that the colours could then be applied as little more than flat areas of paint.

7 Moving on to the second figure, I used the same approach to apply its colour. I also used a temporary flat colour for each of their neck ties, as I knew that I was going to apply a scanned texture to those in just a minute. I'd already introduced a texture to the left figure's waistcoat at this stage. I darkened the background even more at this point to try and get more of a feel for the lighting and mood.

8 Next, I scanned patterned textiles to use for the clothing of the two characters. First of all, I dragged each texture into the image, between the line layer and the paint layer. Using the *Lasso* tool, I then made a very quick selection of the neck tie and followed this by using a hard-edged brush in *Quick Mask* mode to more carefully refine the selection. With the selection inversed, I erased the surplus texture outside of the tie area. For the tie of the figure on the left – if I am to reveal all the grisly details of this production – I scanned in a pair of patterned underpants. They just seemed to lend themselves quite well to the neckwear of an eminent Victorian scientist. I finished this all up by painting on a few highlights to give the previously flat texture some appropriate folds. With the second character's tie texture selected, I applied a slight gradient from the top to accentuate the suggestion of light from below. I adjusted the colour of the textures using *Color Balance* and *Hue/Saturation*, and also their contrast using *Contrast/Brightness*. When I was sure that I had the textures working convincingly on the figures, I merged them both onto the paint layer. Finally, I saved the selections in case there was a need to adjust them later.

9 I now tidied up the figures by tying all of the different elements together, and by adding in any finishing touches. For a change to my normal working practice, I was determined to loosen up and leave the figures a little bit rough around the edges, and not get caught up in refining them to an ultra-smooth finish. I deliberately left any stray lines that might be visible here or there. This less fussy approach is something I'd been enjoying with the large number of concept drawings that I'd been doing prior to starting on this picture. I adjusted the figures by using the *Color Balance* and *Hue/Saturation* menus to give them a greener pallor. I also increased the saturation of the background colour at this point, using *Hue/Saturation*. I wanted to introduce more of a toxic green, but I also wanted to experiment with bringing in my background imagery as a layer in *Multiply* mode – allowing the green to filter through to tint the scene.

13 Now for the final touches. With all of the layers flattened, I added a few touches where any especially untidy joins between the elements were visible, and used the *Blur* tool to soften the edges of certain things, including the outlines of the two characters. This helped blend it together more. Finally, I applied a very slight *Distort > **Spherize*** filter, to accentuate the impression of looking through imperfect glass.

The end result wasn't exactly what I'd initially envisaged, but it's rarely the case that I achieve what I set out to do, and that's obviously part of the fun. Still, the image to some extent manages to convey the mood I wanted, as these two dabbling scientists discover all 'man was never meant to know'. May God have mercy upon their souls!

All in all, I thought the result was moderately successful, and would probably bring that little bit more to the development of *Frankenstein's Legions*.

10 Now that I was satisfied with the figures, I began work on the background. I constructed this in black and white on a new layer, rapidly painting in a stone wall backdrop to suggest a gloomy interior. Against this, I worked-in a piece of weird test-tube-like apparatus, not really having any idea what it might be except that it created the right Frankenstein-lab vibe. Other objects included a headless cadaver in one corner, and some bottles, a book pile, and a chain extending up into the gloom. All of these things were intended to indicate what sort of clichéd horror territory we were in.

11 I wanted to find out if the 'looking out of the tank' view was going to work, and I was keen to quickly introduce a suggestion of the goo contained in the tank. So it was that I found myself photographing a pint glass full of bubbly dilute washing-up liquid. I used the macro setting on my digital camera to capture some of that close-up bubble detail. Dragging this latest addition onto the scene as the topmost layer, I transformed the photograph to fill the frame, set the layer to *Lighten* mode at a little under 100% *Opacity*, and adjusted its *Hue/Saturation* and *Brightness/Contrast*.

12 For the reflection, I painted in a pair of eyes and some teeth on a new layer. It was difficult to know what to do with the face to explain the scientists' shock, given that they'd obviously already been tampering with unnatural forces with some abandon. I just thought if the face looked reasonably evil and hostile, it might be sufficient. I set the layer to *Luminosity* mode at 30% *Opacity*, making the reflection appear translucent. I also added a few small blood stains to the shirt of the right-hand figure to make it look like he's been busy working on other messy parts of their creation.

Howling

IN THE SECOND OF HIS TUTORIALS, Roberto Campus demonstrates his painting techniques within Photoshop, and in particular explains the techniques he utilizes to achieve flesh tones quickly using adjustment layers.

'I have always been in love with horror, fantasy and science fiction art, but I did not pursue it seriously until I discovered the art of Boris Vallejo and Frank Frazetta during my late teenage years. In my early 20s, I put all my energies into learning and practising with traditional media and painting in oils, in an effort to acquire a solid foundation.

I later transferred this knowledge to the digital realm. My style is very flexible, changing from a very realistic look to a more painterly feel. In most of my artwork, you will find strong light sources, glowing effects and the heavy use of highlights. Lately, all of my professional work has been done digitally, because it allows for generally faster production time. My clients generally include comic and role-playing game publishers, as well as computer game and trading card game companies.

'This illustration was originally intended to be used as a heavy metal band's CD album cover. Unfortunately, the deal fell through before I had a chance to start painting it, but I liked the concept so I decided to go ahead and create it anyway, as an addition to my portfolio. I didn't have much time to work on this since my schedule was busy as usual with comic colouring projects. In total I spent about eight hours on it, spread over a few days. The subject matter is one that I was very fond of at the time: Demons.'

SOFTWARE **PHOTOSHOP** ARTIST **ROBERTO CAMPUS** WEBSITE WWW.ROBERTOCAMPUS.COM EMAIL BOB@ROBERTOCAMPUS.COM

1 The sketching was done at low resolution at 72dpi for speed. It is important to stress that, for me at least, the faster that a sketch can be completed, then the better it will be. I find that the best approach for me is to let the shapes flow from my hand to the screen without much interference. If I were to stop every few strokes, then I would lose the spontaneity that is the key to a successful sketch. I made several sketches in quick succession, all slightly different and all drawn on a new blank layer. I try to keep a constant brush size to avoid wasting time on sketching in any details, which at this initial stage can be a distraction and could get in the way during the next phase.

Once I had a few interesting sketches separated on different layers, I compared them and picked the one I thought better conveyed the idea that I had set out to illustrate.

2 The blocking phase is where I concentrate on defining the volume of the figure: the way the light source (in this case a single spotlight positioned above) illuminates the subjects. To achieve a high level of realism, I decided to take a few reference snapshots with a digital camera. Lacking a model at the time, I posed for the pictures myself. I then imported these photos into Photoshop, *Desaturated* them and added a high level of contrast to maximize the highlights and shadows that I needed to refer to. I resized the reference pictures to a small size and then put them to the left of my main canvas window. I moved back to the sketch window and resized it to 300dpi. I set the sketch layer in *Multiply* mode and added an empty layer below it, which I filled with a black colour. In this new layer, I then painted a flat shape following the edges of the sketch, using a 50% flat grey brush tip. After the 'flat' (a comic book term) was done, I proceeded to build up the shadows in the darker areas using several light strokes. At this point, I deleted the sketch layer. I saved all of the highlights for the next step. While working on the blocking, I never zoomed in closer than 50%, to avoid falling into the trap of getting lost in time-consuming details.

TOOL SETTINGS AND NOTES: *Brushes tool. Normal mode.*
When sketching in Photoshop, I use a medium hardness, pressure-sensitive, round brush with a grey colour. I prefer this brush setting because it allows me to define shapes with clear edges with a few quick strokes.

TOOL SETTINGS AND NOTES: *Brushes tool. Normal mode.*
For this stage of the process, I rely on a 0% hardness (smooth edged), pressure-sensitive brush set at 80% *Opacity*. Having a pressure-sensitive stylus and tablet is very useful when painting an image such as this, where smooth flesh tones are prominent. Once again, I kept the brush size constant through this step until the very end, when I hinted at some of the smaller details.

3 For the main stage of the painting, I zoomed in at 100% and started reshaping the anatomy to bring each muscle and the visible bone structure to more exact and convincing shape and proportions. I didn't spend much time blending the strokes, as the focus here was to add in highlights and lighter tones. For the actual painting, I used a combination of short and light brush strokes while alternating between black and white brush tip colors using the 'x' key (in order for this to work, I set up the brush foreground colour as white and the background colour as black). I accentuated some shapes with darker lines, and also brought to prominence the lightest spots with a few touches of pure white. Often, I zoomed out to get a feel for the overall look of the image. I use keyboard shortcuts constantly – to switch between colours, to undo, to zoom in and out, and so on – so I keep my left hand on the keyboard at all times while painting. Doing so speeds up the process considerably.

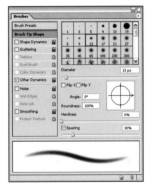

4 Working on the foundation set in the previous step, I used a technique borrowed from oil painting. All of the rough dabs of colour, especially for the highlights, are blended together using the *Smudge* tool. This simulates the way that I paint in oils, where I would build the highlights by putting a small amount of white (or another colour lighter than the base) onto the area that I want to lighten and then blend it and shape it, using a soft-bristled brush. Applying the same method to digital painting is a breeze, especially using Photoshop's *Smudge* tool. This is where I spent the largest amount of time, refining in detail every part of the image. The hardest sections to blend convincingly were the large muscle groups such as the legs and abdominals. I relied here on my knowledge of anatomy – a requirement when you are portraying bodies. While blending, I switched to the *Paint Brush* tool once in a while, whenever I needed an additional touch of white or black. I also zoomed in, up to 300%, to work closely on the small details on the faces. I wanted to maintain a painted feel, so I avoided blending too heavily. After the blending was completed, I used the *Dodge* tool set on *Highlights* to punch up some of the highlights that I felt needed to be stronger, but I used this technique sparingly.

TOOL SETTINGS AND NOTES: *Brushes tool. Normal mode.*
The brush setting I used for this stage is just about the same as the one I employed for the blocking phase, but with slightly increased spacing and *Opacity* varying from 50% to 100%. I continuously adjusted the brush size, depending on the amount of detail that each area required.

SMUDGE TOOL.
Normal mode.
I selected a small, medium-to-high opacity, pressure-sensitive, 0% hardness, round brush for the blending process. It is important to notice that I set the spacing at 30% because a lower spacing would cause the brush tool to perform really slowly and move too much 'paint'.

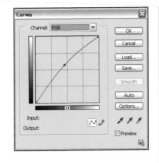

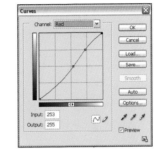

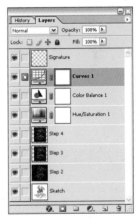

5 At this point, I added colour to the so far still black-and-white painting. Using one of the most powerful features of Photoshop, *Adjustment Layers*, I was able to experiment with different colour schemes until I found the one I was looking for. An advantage of using this method is that I can change the colours at any time, without having to repaint any parts of the illustration.

Here I wanted to give the image a strong dramatic feel and I opted for a palette based on fleshy red tones, for an overall Caravaggio feel.

5a First, I added an *Adjustment* layer to colourize the figures: *Layers > New Adjustment Layer > Hue/Saturation*. I put this above the painting layer, checked the *colorize* button, set the *Hue* to 11, the *Saturation* to 50 and the *Lightness* to 0. The black-and-white figure is now coloured. The colours need further manipulation, however, because the flesh tones are still too uniform.

5b Second, above this I added a *Color Balance Adjustment* Layer as follows: *Layer > New Adjustment Layer > Color Balance*. In the *Shadows* tone balance settings, I moved the *Color level* to –9 on the *Cyan* slider. I left the *Midtones* sliders untouched. In the *Highlights* tone balance settings, I set the *Yellow* slider on –17. This introduced a variation between the darker and lighter colours. It was still not enough.

5c A third modifier was added: *Layers > New Adjustment Layer > Curves*. I used this to add a hint of green to the darker tones, to vary the way the red tones played with the highlights and also to make the picture a bit lighter overall.

Additionally, in order to add more realism to the figure, I used the *Paint Brush* tool to add even more red tones to the figure's cheek, bleeding heart, chest wound, legs and hands.

Flesh tones are hard to obtain, but this method usually allows for a quick shortcut for achieving them.

6 With the main illustration finished, I added my signature logo on a separate layer.

Judge Death: Murder

HAVING BEEN A TECHNOPHOBE for most of his life, Frazer Irving was eventually seduced into the world of digital art, and being able to use a Wacom tablet to draw directly onto virtual canvas, much like with paint brushes, revolutionized his approach to art. As Frazer says, 'Until then, I had resisted colour work due to my inability to make colour choices. But being able to separate colours and elements on layers, and adjust each of them, made the difference.

'I feel the versatility and unpredictability of brushes still far outweighs the digital equivalent. To balance this, I have taken to doing entire strips and illustrations on the computer, but to mimic painted art. Even an image painted in Photoshop using very basic brushes has its own painterly qualities, and this excites me.'

Frazer has worked on various strips for *2000AD* and its sister publication *Megazine*, for which this painted Judge Death cover was created using Photoshop, as he describes in the second of his tutorials. 'This piece was commissioned by Alan Barnes, current editor of the *Judge Dredd Megazine*. I had been hired to draw an eight-part *Judge Death* series, and to coincide with the planned release of the *Dredd vs. Death* computer game, the third episode of that strip would get the cover. The idea was to create two different covers, as a sort of special event, and this allowed me to experiment a little. The first cover idea was an homage to a *Batman* cover from the 1980s. The second cover was my pet project.

'In episode 3, Judge Death encounters a pair of roaming lunatics who are hell-bent on drug abuse and murder. Titled "Natural Born Killers" as a satire on the film of the same name, the story was brutal and surreal. I decided that a pulpy feel was needed to balance the clean, tight art of the first cover and to capture the trashy and brutal nature of the contents.'

SOFTWARE **PHOTOSHOP** ARTIST **FRAZER IRVING** WEBSITE **WWW.FRAZERIRVING.COM** EMAIL **ART@FRAZERIRVING.COM**

4

1 The first step is to make the primary sketch. My initial instinct was to have a predictable image of Death putting his hands through some poor soul's face, probably one of the two main characters. I did my sketches for this cover using the same method that I use for all my work now. This means that I set up a template in Photoshop sized to the print dimensions of the magazine and set at 500dpi in greyscale. Since most magazines print at a maximum of 300dpi, it may seem that going higher than that is wasteful, but I like the freedom that 500dpi gives me when drawing that extra detail. With today's computers, it isn't such a drain on resources to do this. I create a layer in this document and then, using a preset brush tool set to mimic pencil, I sketch the idea very loosely using my oversize A4 Wacom tablet.

2 As with every other cover I draw, I experiment with a variety of different versions of each composition until an idea hits me. With this cover, I hit the magic moment within the first three tries, and this is the result. I decided that having a symbolic triangle with all three main characters was the best option. It was simple and direct, and was also suited to the design of the logo and text placements. During this I also hit upon the idea that I could surround Death's head with an army of his former victims as ghostly portraits, re-affirming his status as a monster mass-murderer. Originally I had the idea that this sketch would then be traced on another layer to make a tighter drawing to paint on, but this wasn't the case mainly due to time constraints.

3 The next step was to set the drawing onto a painted background. I open a new document, again sized to print dimensions but at 500dpi and in RGB mode, and I pasted in a watercolour scan. This is sized to fit and then flattened, giving me a background not unlike one I would create for a real painting. Next, the sketch is pasted in a new layer. I draw into the sketch, making it darker where I need to and changing the position of Death's head. This is done by drawing on a new layer and then simply erasing the previous head and merging the two sketch layers. I also use the Burn tool to burn some tone into the background texture.

4 The first paint was applied almost as an experiment. I have several Custom Brushes, all of which have been constructed from the default brushes in Photoshop. The two I used at this point were my regular painting brush, which is a solid round brush with the *Opacity* set to react to the pen pressure, and a mutated chalk brush designed to mimic thick wet oil paint. I painted the light as it comes from below the characters' heads, and I chose magenta because I wanted garish colours. I applied the paint on one layer above the sketch, picking out just the highlights, allowing the mid-tones of the sketch and the background texture to show through. I added a sickly yellow to the girl's teeth and some off-white to her eyes for definition. The guy's hair was done with the oil paint brush, painted on in much the same way I would with a regular brush. I also added some highlights to Judge Death's hands.

5 The next stage was to add paint to Judge Death. To provide contrast, I went for this ghostly blue. I painted on a new layer and instantly saw the colours arguing with each other, which was exactly the effect that I wanted. I used a third brush at this point, which was a variation on the *Chalk* brush from Photoshop, because I wanted to create a slightly chalky texture to Judge Death.

6 I created a new layer and painted on a secondary light source. Originally I had it reflecting on all three characters, but I figured that it worked best when it was just on Judge Death because it created a much better sense of depth.

I played around with the colours of all three of the colour layers here, as I wasn't convinced that they would work together. Using the *Hue/Saturation* tool, this was pretty easy, but in the end I decided to leave such decisions until later.

7 Another layer is created and I now move on to draw Judge Death's face. This would be a major focal point for the image, so I wanted to spend a bit of time and get the detail in.

As with the other two characters, I decided that just painting the highlights and leaving the shadows to the sketch/background would create a sufficiently ghostly feel to his face, so I picked out his helmet grille, his teeth and chin and that was it. I used my chalk brush for this on the whole.

9 Following on with my original idea, I made a new layer and drew the faces of Death's previous victims, using the sketch layer as a guide for placement. To facilitate this, I had to make use of my keyboard actions. I have set up my F-keys to play out important actions, and in this case I used the rotate action to spin the art around so that I could draw in the faces of those people on the sides and the bottom. While this is good enough, I still yearn for Painter's flexibility in this regard, where one can rotate the canvas freehand to any angle one desires; just like real paper.

10 Here I created another new layer so that I could add the white needed to bring some life to the ghosts in Death's background. Not much detail was required here, so the faces all took just small drops of white to add a third level of depth to them. As well as this, I need to bring out the heads as a group, so I used the *Chalk* and *Brush* tools to paint between the heads. Overall, I was very pleased with the result. It was a very simple method in comparison to many previous covers, and I managed to create a fair replica of a real painting – and all within a single day.

8 Next I had to decide what the background would be. I couldn't leave it simply as the watercolour texture (much as I liked it) and so I decided to start by painting in the whole space with one colour. I used my oil paint brush and picked the colour closest to Death, then I proceeded to paint in freehand on a new layer. Doing this not only removed the distraction of the background texture, but it also defined the edges of the foreground figures and settled the colour contrast. Once the backing colour was painted in, I knew that I wanted to stick with these colours.

This version of the image is still my favourite, mainly because of its simplicity. Here I can see the two main figures as condemned souls, the fiery light of hell illuminating them from below while Judge Death rises like some ghostly grim reaper from a cold, damp pocket of the underworld. This captured the feel I wanted and had all the narrative elements I felt were important, but this is publishing and the shelves demand a different type of image.

Elder Daemons

DAVE CARSON HAS BEEN a fan of horror films for as long as he can remember, leaning in the direction of monster and supernatural films, and these have been a great influence on his work. His art has appeared in many publications over the years, including the excellent *Dragon* magazine, Chaosium's *Call of Cthulhu* game, Games Workshop's *White Dwarf* magazine, and the 'Fighting Fantasy' book *Beneath Nightmare Castle*. The influence of H. P. Lovecraft looms heavily throughout all of his work, and he quotes Lovecraft's tale *The Call of Cthulhu* as his favourite piece by the master of supernatural horror.

In this demonstration, Dave uses relatively simple 2D and 3D techniques in an attempt to replicate the style of his traditional black-and-white drawings for which he's renowned. He aimed for something of the feel he achieves when sculpting in stone – a process in which he often incorporates found objects. This is echoed digitally in his use of ready-made 3D objects.

Dave mentioned a few useful packages. 'Amorphium is a 3D sculpting program in which you can mould and shape practically any 3D object like a piece of clay, and it's relatively easy to use. Bryce is a handy tool as well, and in my opinion greatly underrated. It can be used to produce landscapes, seascapes, clouds, simple 3D models and more. One drawback is that it can impart a very recognizable "Bryce" look if it is overused – so subtlety is paramount. Spiralizer is a handy freeware application that can create 3D models of spirally things in general. That's about all it does, but it does it well.

'3ds max was used only very briefly here to create a few simple tentacles for the creature in the background. It has a fairly steep learning curve, and quite honestly I don't have the inclination to get involved with such powerful and time-consuming software.'

Copyright © 2003 Dave Carson

SOFTWARE PHOTOSHOP, AMORPHIUM, BRYCE, 3DS MAX, SPIRALIZER ARTIST DAVE CARSON EMAIL FROMHELL@BTOPENWORLD.COM

4

1 Starting with a plain black canvas in Photoshop, I added the doorway from an old photo and combined this with a simple wooden floor surface produced in Bryce by laying an aged wooden plank texture out on the horizontal plane. I laid over this some organic-looking textures taken from my own photographs of lichen, eroded stone, and so on, and then adjusted the layer *Transparency* to suit. Some smoky effects were then added, using a blend of cloud photographs.

I then combined all of these layers together to create the background of the image.

2 For the mounds of human remains, a small pile of bones was rendered in Bryce, using various 3D models of ribcages, skulls and whatever else came to hand. This layer was duplicated in Photoshop, distorted here and there, resized and *Transformed*, duplicated again, and so on, until I had enough different-looking layers to combine into the heaps of bones for my background.

3 The foreground creature was made up from separate, small, organic and bony looking shapes created in Amorphium, given a nice texture and rendered in Bryce, then laboriously pieced together on separate layers in Photoshop to form various extrusions and body parts. A model of a human skull came in handy here — suitably distorted in Amorphium. All of the demons in the image were created by the same method, apart from the tentacled thing rising behind the pile of bones on the left. This was made from a simple organic shape created in Amorphium for the body, with the addition of some tentacles created in 3ds max. The process is very similar to the way that I make a sculpture, combining found objects with pieces carved by hand — the objects here either being obtained as free objects from the Internet or created specifically for the job.

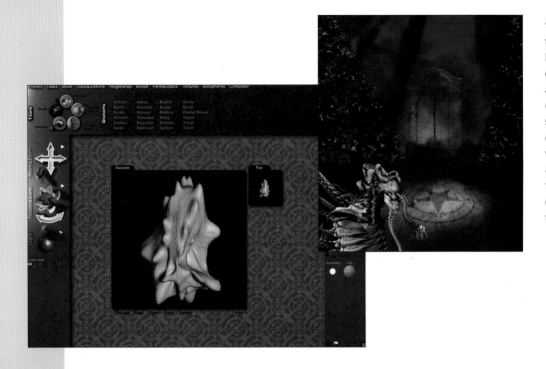

4 The rays of light breaking through from above were added by simply *Masking* out the shape of the rays on a separate layer and then adding a simple white *Gradient* in Photoshop and a slight *Gaussian Blur* to soften the edges. The *Opacity* of the layer was then adjusted to the correct amount. The pentagram on the floor is simply a scanned image distorted with the *Transform* tool to give it some perspective.

5 The guttering candles came from a collection of royalty-free images included on a magazine freebie CD. I masked them off, added *Lens Flare* slightly to the tops of each of them and then used the *Smudge* tool in Photoshop to create the smoke.

6 All of the other creatures that I had created earlier and kept on separate layers were finally placed into the image and moved around until I was happy with the positioning.

7 Finally, everything is tidied up. I darkened down the background slightly, and then went through the other layers to adjust their lightness or darkness, and repositioned the various layers slightly until I felt everything was as good as it was going to get.

Elder Daemons was a non-commissioned piece, and actually originated as an experiment in creating a single demon creature from organic 3D shapes in Amorphium and Bryce in an attempt to make my computer

work reflect the look and style of my black and white line work. It was really just a bit of experimentation to begin with. I continued adding to it and ended up with quite a menagerie of demons, which eventually I realized I could do something more ambitious with. I decided to go for a dimly-lit subterranean scene with a suggestion of light breaking through cracks in the unseen floor above, and strewn with the skeletal remains of ghastly demonic sacrificial feasts. I was pleased with the result, as it turned out to be the closest I've come digitally to the eldritch look that I'm used to in my black-and-white illustrations.

Ghosthunter: Junkyard Robot

ANGELO BOD IS A SENIOR ARTIST AT Sony Computer Entertainment Europe's Cambridge studio (SCEE). He has been involved with games since 1983, but started his career as a professional artist in 1989. Angelo has worked on an impressive list of titles from the 8-bit to next generation consoles, covering different platforms such as the Super Nintendo, Sega Dreamcast, Philips CDi, Atari ST, Commodore Amiga, PC and Sony PlayStation. Some of the recent projects Angelo has worked on include *Plague*, *Deathtrap Dungeon* and *Blood Omen 2* for Eidos Interactive; *European Super League* for Virgin Interactive; *Final Fantasy X* for Squaresoft; *Beach King Stunt Racer* and *US Racer* for Davilex Games – and the PlayStation2 game *Ghosthunter* for SCEE, from which this tutorial's artwork is derived.

In this step-by-step example, Angelo takes us through the creation of a promotional image for the horror-themed computer game *Ghosthunter*, using Maya to produce his 3D characters, and then Photoshop for the textures and the final composition.

Rendered image for promotional use. Production still based on the game Ghosthunter™ for the Playstation®2 © Sony Computer Entertainment Europe.

THE ARTWORK

The purpose of this image was to create high-resolution artwork to promote the horror game *Ghosthunter* in magazines and other print media. It was decided that the scene should show the main character in the game, Lazarus, confronting one of the game's most memorable and horrific villains – a huge and murderous robot composed of junk metal. The high-resolution model of the Lazarus character had already been created by Jason Riley, who also worked on the evil Teddy Monster for *Ghosthunter*. And the robot itself had originally been conceived and designed by artist Jason Wilson.

1 I began work on the image with the creation of a new high-resolution version of the Junkyard Robot, as the low-resolution version (which had been created previously) was only for real-time in-game use on the PlayStation2, and not suitable for appearance in print. The in-game model was approximately 6000 polygons. For the new model, I used a combination of NURBS and polygons. And as I had to imagine this huge 24-metre high monster was mainly built from metal, I used a lot of metallic texture maps with bump, specular and diffuse-maps. The resolution for these individual maps was 1024 x 1024 pixels.

SOFTWARE ALIAS WAVEFRONT MAYA 4.5 ADOBE PHOTOSHOP 7.01 WONDERTOUCH PARTICLE ILLUSION ARTIST ANGELO BOD, SONY COMPUTER ENTERTAINMENT EUROPE, COPYRIGHT 2003 WEBSITE WWW.ANGELOBOD.COM EMAIL INFO@ANGELOBOD.COM

2 For reference material, I used photographs that I had taken in a scrapyard, which included rusty old cars, washing machines and tyres. I also researched other related materials which I wanted to use in this composition, including effects like smoke and flames. I used the in-game model as a template to create the high-resolution version, although I remodelled most of the parts, and used a lot of bevelling for the rounded edges. Most Maya users already know to bevel an object before the creation of the UV maps for the model. This is one feature I hope will be fixed in the near future.

The main objects needed in this image were: the lead character from the game, Lazarus; one of the weapons that he has available from his armoury within the game itself; the Junkyard Robot model; and a suitable background. The background I used in some of the test shots was the real-time junkyard model from the game, which was a pretty large model environment, but once again of insufficient resolution for print. If I had chosen to use this background in the final art, I would still have had to remodel the object from scratch and redo its textures – due to the same resolution issues that meant I had to remodel the Junkyard Robot.

3 The Lazarus figure had already been modelled by the artist Jason Riley, so the only thing that was needed was for the model to have a skin applied before posing him in the required position. The process of skinning can be fairly complex, but as you do it more often it obviously becomes more of a routine job, just like everything else. This consists of placing all of the joints into the right positions anatomically and making sure that all of the joints are pointing in the right direction and so on. I used smooth bind for skinning, and started painting the weights into the model.

I had to keep all of the details of his appearance consistent with the in-game version, so I had to give the character one of the weapons that he carries in the game. I had six firearms to choose from, all of which had been fully designed and modelled prior to my beginning work on this image. Here are three of them – the Grenade Launcher, Hoover Gun and the Sniper Rifle. These were made separately for marketing purposes and for appearance in the manual to accompany the game. Some of the close-up images of the weapons here will show you the amount of detail that we put into them. These images were all rendered using the Maya renderer.

4 But which weapon should Lazarus be carrying in this scene – his confrontation with the huge Junkyard Robot? I decided to make his fight seem even more futile, and kind of funny, by giving him a small handgun – his chances of defeating the junkyard monster now seem even more unlikely!

4

5 For the Junkyard Robot, all of the textures for this huge 24-metre-high piece of scrap metal had to be re-created due to the print size, keeping in mind the final image could be as little as 15,000 pixels in height. The textures in-game were as high as 128 x 128 pixels.

As I mentioned before, I used photographs from a real junkyard featuring various metallic objects, including cars and washing machines, and so on. Over the years, I have slowly built up a library of various photographs, which is always coming in handy.

Using the Internet for finding reference material is also a fantastic new technology, but it's usually insufficient because most of the time the best images are either copyrighted, or at too low a resolution to use for anything that is intended for print – although photo reference material suitable for in-game textures can be found quite readily.

6 Making use of Photoshop's *Rubber Stamp* tool, I can fairly quickly manipulate an image to create a texture of the exact size that I need. Sometimes there are imperfections in a photo or even just parts of it that I want to remove. To do this, I use the *Rubber Stamp* tool to smooth out any parts that I don't want on a texture, so that its surface is exactly like I need it. After that, I have to decide if I'll use the texture as a tile – horizontal, vertical or both. In the right-hand texture shown above, I wanted to create a metal surface with some detail of rust and nails clearly visible. On the first layer, the texture is cleaned up by using the *Rubber Stamp* tool, and I made it tileable by using the *Offset* tool and *Rubber Stamp* again. On the second layer, I used a texture with some of the detail that I wanted, adding this

as a *Normal* layer, but with an *Opacity* of 53%. Finally, on the third layer, I placed a copy of the texture that I used on the first layer. The flattened image on the right is one of the final textures I used on the Junkyard Robot model. All of the scrap metal on the Junkyard Robot's head is fully modelled, as simply using plain objects with *Alpha* maps didn't achieve the effect that I wanted.

A wireframe & solid pose shot taken from the Junkyard Robot model.

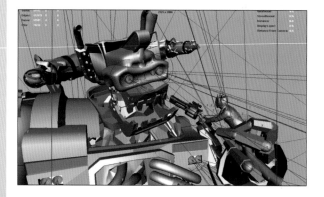

7 After finishing the modelling and texturing, I started to add lights to parts of the model, defining the positioning of the various wrecked vehicles that were incorporated into its construction – their beams shooting in different directions to

add interest. On the model, 22 lights were used. Using *Spotlights* with a high intensity, linear *Decay* and some other parameters, I created a light that simulated a slight noise when rendering and would cast and reflect off surrounding objects.

Pose shot in shaded view in Maya. The blue lines represent the spotlights.

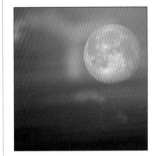

Render of the final Junkyard Robot model, using the Maya renderer. No *Radiosity* or *Global Illumination* was used here.

8 Before creating the final image, I posed some test shots of the Junkyard Robot, along with the figure of Lazarus and elements of the background.

From this point on, I had all the models ready to position within the scene. The objective was to create a close-up of the Junkyard Robot seen together with Lazarus in one shot. About 14 shots were staged and quick-rendered to get an impression of which one I wanted to develop fully. Some of the influences were images from *2000AD* and *The Iron Giant*. As Lazarus was tiny compared to this huge metal monster, and they both had to be prominent in the image, I tried several poses. At first, I showed Lazarus kneeling and hiding from the metal monster. But as this wasn't very heroic, I decided to go for a close-up of Lazarus attacking the Junkyard Robot head-on. I still think it's funny to see Lazarus impossibly attacking the Junkyard Robot with an ordinary handgun.

9 After the best composition was approved, I started working out what else I needed, and what kind of environment I wanted the scene to be set in. What special effects would I need – smoke, fire, rain, etc.? I used the Internet for my research to get an idea of smoke, light effects, etc., and any images that I could refer to, which I could maybe draw from to add realism to the scene.

10 I needed to render the images in separate layers, so that I could add details such as rain, smoke, fire and light effects afterwards. Also, I needed to allow some flexibility in the image, just in case things had to be moved around to suit a cover layout later.

Breaking this image down in Photoshop reveals five main layers. Some parts had to be masked because of the lights and smoke effects, which were put into the image separately.

The uppermost layer is the render of the Junkyard Robot, where I had to mask areas for adding smoke and light effects at a later stage. The second layer is for emphasizing the light effect the Junkyard Robot is casting onto itself and its environment – this was also done using masks. The third layer is·a render of Lazarus. On the fourth layer, there's the smoke effect and some shading masks. The smoke effects were partly drawn within Photoshop, and I also used Particle Illusion to create the smoke coming out of the Junkyard Robot's exhaust pipes. I used a template and started tweaking the particles so I could use them in this layer – keeping the transparency from the rendered particle images. For the fire, I used the same combination of particle effects but made the particles black. The fire was drawn in at a later stage, using photographic reference.

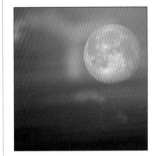

11 The background image was the fifth and bottom layer of the composite. I wanted to keep the focus on the two characters, so I kept it fairly simple, just a creepy monochromatic night sky with a very prominent full moon. After all of the layers were merged together, I converted the image into greyscale so that I could check the contrast and then adjusted the levels within Photoshop to finish everything.

Ghosthunter: Teddy Monster

JASON RILEY CREATES IN-GAME graphics, cinematics and presentation visuals for Sony Computer Entertainment Europe's Cambridge studio (SCEE). His background is in life science and technical illustration and he has been working in the computer games industry since 1993. In the early days, he created 2D sprite animations and backgrounds for games such as *Diggers* and *Silverload* (for Millennium Interactive, 1993 and 1995) and *Creatures* (CyberLife Technology, 1996). *Creatures* was one of the first artificial intelligence games ever made. Jason started working in 3D in 1996 for the PlayStation1 game *MediEvil* (SCEE, 1998) which was his first opportunity to work on full motion video (FMV) using high-end Silicon Graphics workstations. Since then, he's directed and created backgrounds for *Speed Freaks* (Funcom, 1999), *MediEvil II* (BAFTA Award Winner for Best Console Game, SCEE, 2000) and *Primal* (SCEE, 2003) as well as producing high-resolution poster art, magazine spreads and shop front stands.

In this tutorial, Jason takes us through the creation of a promotional image for the *Ghosthunter* computer game, using Maya to create the models in 3D, and then switching to Photoshop for the 2D elements.

'Contrasting subject matter tends to catch the eye in imagery. The very first rolling credit sequence of *Terminator 2* had shots of an innocent-looking playground engulfed by fierce flames from a nuclear explosion. Disturbing, but powerful. This premise formed the basis to some of the characters in *Ghosthunter*.

'The game's lead artist Jason Wilson originally designed the Teddy Monster. It was by far the most memorable character of the game, because of its divergent elements. How could something so cuddly and warm, adored by children, be transformed into a vile, evil beast?'

Rendered image for promotional use. Production still based on the game Ghosthunter™ for the Playstation®2 © Sony Computer Entertainment Europe.

SOFTWARE MAYA, PHOTOSHOP ARTIST JASON RILEY, SONY COMPUTER ENTERTAINMENT EUROPE, COPYRIGHT 2003
WEBSITE WWW.GHOSTHUNTER-GAME.COM

MAKING PROMOTIONAL PRODUCTION STILLS

After two or three years spent creating a game, the marketing department requires an artist from the production team to create high-resolution images to promote and sell the game through magazine covers and articles, shop front stands, television adverts, shows and other paraphernalia.

If I do a magazine cover, I'm always required to make a Photoshop layered format (PSD) file so that the magazine's layout artist can change the cropping, position of objects, scale, and even colour of the final result, so that it complements their text. Magazines tend to overlap certain elements of the image over text to make it more exciting. Without layers, this would take the layout artist a lot of time to cut out or colour separately. If a character needed to move in the foreground by just two pixels, it would have to be sent back to me to be re-rendered. Having layers ensures that the image remains easy to manipulate.

Layers are used all the time in the film industry, because a complex shot requires various specialist companies to provide different effects. For example, one SFX house would do a layer of a character, another effects house may do smoke, flames or particle effects. This works as long as the camera angles are established right at the beginning of the project.

1 Even though it will be a CG image, I still have to think like a traditional painter. Colour, depth, mood, tone, proportion, composition and balance all contribute to a great image. Firstly, I have to present a preliminary sketch to the magazine publisher.

2 The publisher promptly sends a version back with a rough cut of their intended text overlay. The tonal sketch is then drawn, entirely for my benefit so that I can establish the appropriate levels of light and dark, create an illusion of space and make sure that there is a good balance in the composition. The boundary of the picture has been defined, but I still usually allow a 2–3cm bleed to give the magazine a little extra room for manoeuvre.

4

3 Once the preliminary sketches have been finalized, the final 3D image can be formed, starting with the background. I model solid straight-lined, static objects in polygons and soft, organic, flowing components in NURBS or subdivision surfaces. The aim is to create something that is amazing, with as little render time and workflow cost as possible. I like to try to strike a balance between using as few 3D points (vertices) as I possibly can, while maintaining the quality of the image.

Background components require very little 3D point detail. If it's further away, it won't be noticed! A back wall would probably have just four points, for example. A foreground wall would probably have a few hundred vertices, to show the chips, cracks and weathering.

My foreground objects always have fine bevelled edges. I try to stop things having that hard, sharp-edged, CG look to them, as in reality things rarely do. I add extra details like wood splinters, bird feathers resting on wood beams, and pigeon and bat droppings on to colour and bump maps.

4 The foreground elements' wire frames are coloured yellow. These will be separated and rendered after the back and middle grounds have been finished.

Once I have established a camera angle, I have to stick to it and use the same viewpoint on all layers. The camera angle is saved and locked so that it doesn't move. The same applies to the lighting system.

In Maya, the Teddy's fur will render most successfully in spotlights. I then have to consider positions of both natural and artificial light sources, which will set the atmosphere and seem life-like. There's the main moonlight source streaming through a gap in the rafters, which casts a bright highlight on the floor. From here, the light is bounced and diffused all over the room. I created a very wide spotlight for this ambient effect. There's a torchlight, and a reddish fill-light to add a little warm definition to the foreground objects. This helps to bring them forward and prevent their appearing like silhouettes. I will render the fog on the lights later on a separate layer as a final touch.

To create accurate shadows, reflections and refractions, I ray-trace my renders. I like to use radial, soft shadows which are costly in terms of calculation time, but are worth it for the results they give. If I have a tight deadline, I tend to use Ray Cast's cast shadows as they render more quickly. These shadows are okay, but they don't have a precise diffusion and shaded quality, and tend to be flat. If time is not an issue, I will venture into Mental Ray, and use radiosity for outstanding realism.

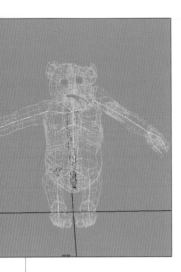

7 This shows my first render of the fur, which obviously needs pruning! Maya has about 23 different *Fur Attributes* to play with, including baldness, hair length, direction and colour.

5 Once again, the Teddy has very few vertices. Easy and quick to manage, points are a base wireframe bound to a smoothed, sub-divided mesh underneath.

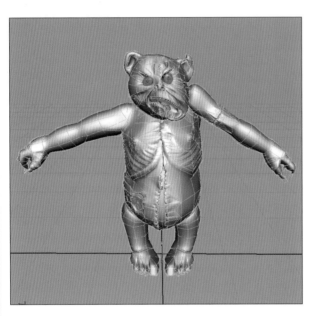

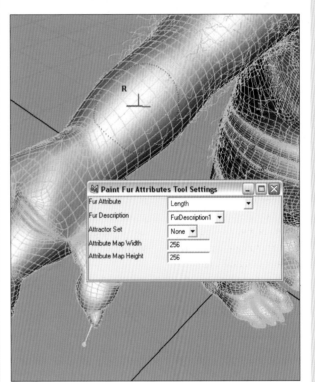

6 The Teddy will be attached to a virtual skeleton, which gives it realistic working joints.

Notice how the Teddy was fixed to the joints in an 'arms out' pose, called a bind pose.

Technically this is the best way to ensure that all joints are in the correct position. I will hide the base mesh, keeping the sub-division surface visible, and then attach some fur to it.

8 I can physically use a 3D tool in Maya called *Artisan*, which strokes over the surface of the character, updating the fur feedback in real time. For the Teddy's full body of fur, I ended up using a staggering 400,000 follicles of hair. When Maya renders this, it draws the naked bear first, and then literally a few seconds later, it draws the fur result on top. Before you apply the fur to the mesh, it is very important that the mesh's texture coordinates are first unwrapped (flattened out) and then neatly arranged in a texture square. This process is called UV mapping.

4

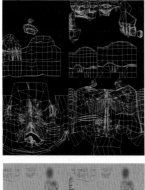
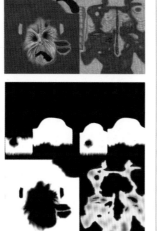
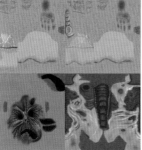

9 In the top-left corner is a snapshot of my UV layout of the Teddy. This will be my template for adding the texture to. Most of the time, I paint my textures in Photoshop. It is possible to paint onto the 3D surface in Maya (using *Artisan*), but I use Photoshop for additional speed and control to create a colour map (shown in the top-right). I think about the blood layer underneath the skin, the vein layer, the blotches and the crinkly

texture. Even though the Teddy is covered in fur, I still have to consider the surface below in case it's exposed in the image.

After this colour map is finished, I use this as reference for the bump map (bottom-left) and add faint white lines that represent the vascular veins. In the bottom-right corner is a mask to stop the translucency value of the skin in a render from breaking through the brown fur muslin detail.

10 In the final image, the Teddy's reflection in the mirror had to be rendered on a separate layer from the 'real' Teddy, since fur can't yet be reflected with this package. I matched the perspective of the floor plane to that of the reflection in the mirror of the background image.

If there are any glitches in the render, like broken polygons here and there, I will cheat and paint them out wherever possible. There

are always one or two human errors in this kind of work, but from around 30,000 polygons, that's not too bad!

It's quite common to go into the picture with the trusty paint brush and alter things on the surface. I often use *Smear* to break up straight lines, or I might add more highlights and darken areas. Such techniques are commonly used for getting the job done efficiently.

4

1   2   3   4   5   6   7

11 Here is the multi-layered format PSD file in use. Every layer is easy to change, or replace: if, say, the client doesn't like the posture of the Teddy, then he is quickly altered, without having to render him with the background again. If the client doesn't like too much fog, this can be changed instantly. So what happens to Teddy after this picture? He's already skinned up ready for anything; animation, more marketing pictures, T-shirts, who knows? The background and its objects could be altered or used again from a different camera angle shot. From time to time, I grab objects from an existing scene and insert them into a new one. I've been in the industry a long time, and have created quite a library of stuff.

Who's gonna know?

A TYPICAL PHOTOSHOP LAYERED DIAGRAM

1. Foreground. Rendered in Maya, using *Paint Effects* for the paper stuffing. The shadows were *Alpha Channelled* using *Use Background* shader.
2. Small Ted, again taking advantage of the *Use Background* shader.
3. In a separate Maya file of the scene, I coloured all of the 3D data black and rendered the blue light ray effect from the moon. The Photoshop layer will be a screen overlay, meaning the darker the colour, the more transparent it will become.
4. The same effect as used on layer three, but this one shows the fog depth. I also use this layer as an *Alpha Channel* for layer number five.
5. Focus map.
6. The sharp background.
7. The Teddy's reflection.

Glossary

16-BIT COLOUR
A facility in image-editing applications that allows you to work on images in 16-bit-per-channel mode, rather than eight, allowing finer control over colour, but larger file sizes. An RGB image would total 48 bits (16 x 3) and a CMYK image 64 bits (16 x 4).

24-BIT COLOUR
Allocating 24 bits of memory to each pixel, giving a screen display of 16.7 million colours (a row of 24 bits can be written in 16.7 million different combinations of 1s and 0s), sometimes called true-colour. Twenty-four bits are required for CMYK separations (eight bits for each).

ALPHA CHANNEL
Pixel channel used to store data such as mask or transparency information. Appears as a separate greyscale channel, which accompanies any image file and determines which parts of the final image are affected.

BLEND(ING)
A merging of two or more colours, forming a gradual transition from one to the other. The quality of the blend is limited by the number of shades of a single colour that can be reproduced without visible banding.

BMP
Windows file format for bitmapped or pixel-based images.

BUMP MAP
A surface material that adds 'bump' or depth detail to the surface of a model without actually affecting its geometry.

CHROMA
The intensity, or purity, of a colour; thus its degree of saturation.

CLIPPING
Limiting an image or a piece of art to within the bounds of a particular area.

COLOUR GAMUT / SPACE
The full range of colours that are achievable by any single device in the reproduction chain. While the colour spectrum contains many millions of colours, not all are producable by all devices.

COLOUR PICKER
A colour model displayed on a computer monitor, which may be specific to either an application, or to your operating system.

COLOUR TEMPERATURE
The temperature – measured in degree Kelvin – to which a black object would have to be heated to produce a specific colour of light.

CMYK (CYAN, MAGENTA, YELLOW, AND KEY PLATE)
The four-colour printing process based on the subtractive colour model. Black is represented by the letter K, which stands for key plate. In theory, cyan, magenta and yellow when combined form black, but in the printing process this is difficult to achieve and expensive, hence the additional use of the black ink.

CONTROL VERTICES (CVS)
Handles that are used to pull a curve into a more fluid, organic shape, used most often with Bézier curves. CVs do not lie on the curve itself, but 'float' above the surface of it.

CURVES
Adjustment parameter in image-editing applications that allows precise control of the entire tonal range of an image.

DENSITY RANGE
The maximum range of tones of an image, measured as the difference between the darkest and lightest tones.

DODGE
A technique originating in photography which when applied lightens up parts of an image. The dodge tool is found in many 2D image editing applications.

EXTRUSION
The method of creating a 3D object from a 2D path.

HIERARCHY
Tree structure listing objects in a scene or materials on a object, in order to display the logical relationships between them.

LAYERS
Used in many software applications, layers allow you to work on one element of an image without disturbing the others.

LEVELS
Adjustment parameter in image-editing applications that allows the user to correct the tonal range and colour balance of an image by adjusting intensity levels of the image's shadows, midtones, and highlights.

LOFT(ING)
Lofting is where a surface is applied to a series of profile curves that define a frame.

LOSSLESS COMPRESSION
Methods of file compression in which little or no data is lost.

LOSSY COMPRESSION
File compression where data is irretrievably lost. JPEG is an example of a lossy format.

METABALLS
Used in 3D modeling, these are spheres that blend into each other.

NURBS
Stands for Non-Uniform Rational B-Splines – a technique for interactively modelling 3D curves and surfaces.

OMNI LIGHT
Illumination source that points in all directions.

PARENT

An object that is linked to another (known as a child) in a modelling hierarchy. When the parent object moves, the child object moves with it.

PERSPECTIVE

A technique of rendering 3D objects on a 2D plane, by giving the impression of an object's relative position and size when viewed from a particular point.

PIXEL

A contraction of 'picture element'. The smallest component of any digitally generated image, such as a single dot of light on a computer screen. In its simplest form, one pixel corresponds to a single bit: 0=off, or white; 1=on, or black. In colour or greyscale images, one pixel may correspond to up to 24 bits.

POLYGON

The building blocks of 3D on a computer. A number of connected points that together create a shape or face. Polygonal meshes are created from joining these faces together. These meshes then form geometric shapes.

PRIMITIVES

Simple geometrical objects in 3D applications such as spheres, cubes and cylinders, which are combined together or deformed to create more complex shapes.

PSD

Stands for Photoshop Document. Image format for files created using Adobe Photoshop.

RASTERIZE

To electronically convert a vector-based graphics image into a bitmapped image.

RAY TRACING

Rendering procedure which sends out hypothetical rays of light originating from the objects in a scene in order to determine the appearance of each pixel that will appear in the final image.

REFLECTION MAP

A surface material that is used to determine what is reflected in an object's surface

RENDER / RENDERING

The application of textures and lighting, which together transform a collection of objects into a realistic scene. All of the data in the 3D scene - the location and nature of all light sources, locations and shape of all geometry, and also the location and orientation of the camera through which that scene is viewed - are collected to create a fully-realised 2D image.

REVOLVE (TOOL)

This creates a surface from a profile curve that revolves around a defined axis.

RGB (RED, GREEN, BLUE)

The colours of the additive colour model, used on monitors and therefore in Web graphics.

SHADERS

Shaders determine the appearance of an object. These are layers of attributes that make up how the surface of the model reacts to light, colour, reflectivity, appearance and so on.

SMOOTHING

In drawing and 3D applications, smoothing is the refinement of paths or polygons.

SPECULAR

The 'highlight value' of a shiny object, also commonly used in the creation of specular maps.

SPOTLIGHT

Illumination from a single source in one specific direction, along a cone-shaped path.

SUBDIVISION SURFACES

Geometric surface type used for modeling organic objects. Usually built from a polygonal mesh.

TEXTURE MAP

A 2D image (such as a JPG image) used as a shader. Texture maps are applied to the surface of a 3D object in order to give it extra detail, such as scratches and patterns. They can be created inside the 3D application using procedural methods or imported as 2D bitmapped images (file textures) from a digital photo.

TIFF OR TIF

Tagged Image File Format. A standard and popular graphics format used for scanned, high-resolution bitmapped images and colour separations.

TRANSLATION

Manipulation of the position of an object.

TRANSPARENCY MAP

Surface material which determines what is reflected in a transparent object's surface

UV CO-ORDINATES

The vertex co-ordinates of a model that define the surface parameters of an object and therefore enable artists to accurately place parts of an image onto the correct place. (See texture mapping)

UV MAPPING

A way to add a texture map to a 3D polygonal model using the UV co-ordinates.

VECTOR GRAPHICS

Images made up of mathematically defined shapes, or complex paths built out of mathematically defined curves. As a result, they can be resized or displayed at any resolution without loss of quality, but lack the tonal subtlety of bitmaps.

VERTEX

A control point on a path. Often shortened to 'vert'.

VRML

Virtual Reality Modeling Language. An HTML-type programming language designed to create 3D scenes (virtual worlds) on the Internet.

WIREFRAME

A 3D object viewed as a polygonal mesh with no 'surface' or texture applied to it (the object has yet to be rendered). Often used to quickly view a 3D model.

Index

Acknowledgements

Sincere thanks to the artists for all their fantastic contributions, without whom this book simply couldn't have happened.

And special thanks, for all their help and advice, to:

Jim Pritchett, Iain McCaig, Jamie Mathieson, Dave Morris, Leo Hartas, Duncan Oakley, Alex Chapman, Angelo Bod, Robert Weinberg, Ian Livingstone, John Garrett at LucasArts, Christopher Holm at Lucasfilm, Stephen Jones, Jamie Wallis, Dave Carson, Michel Parry, Marc Gascoigne, Simon Flynn.

COPYRIGHT